Supply Chain Optimization through Segmentation and Analytics

Series on Resource Management

RECENT TITLES

Supply Chain Optimization through Segmentation and Analytics

Gerhard J. Plenert

CRC Press
Taylor & Francis Group
Boca Raton   London   New York

CRC Press is an imprint of the
Taylor & Francis Group, an **Informa** business

CRC Press
Taylor & Francis Group
6000 Broken Sound Parkway NW, Suite 300
Boca Raton, FL 33487-2742

Version Date: 20131106

International Standard Book Number-13: 978-1-4665-8476-1 (Hardback)

Library of Congress Cataloging-in-Publication Data

Plenert, Gerhard Johannes.
  Supply chain optimization through segmentation and analytics / Gerhard J. Plenert.
    pages cm. -- (Resource management ; 48)
  Includes bibliographical references and index.
  ISBN 978-1-4665-8476-1
  1. Business logistics. I. Title.

HD38.5.P594 2014
658.7--dc23
                                          2013039554

Visit the Taylor & Francis Web site at
http://www.taylorandfrancis.com

and the CRC Press Web site at
http://www.crcpress.com

To the love of my life—
Renee Sangray Plenert
Who segments my life optimally!
And to my kids, their spouses, and of course the grandkids—
Heidi, Dawn, Gregory and Debby, Gerick and Nicole,
Joshua and Amy, Natasha and Mark, Zackary and Karli,
Chelsey, Lucas, Boston, Evan, Lincoln, Livy,
Savannah, Boston (yes, there really are two with
that name), Beckham, Gerick, Jr., and Gage
Who like to analyze my life!

Contents

SECTION 3   Segmentation Effects

Preface

In a meeting with a COO (Chief Operating Officer) the author was told, "We have had dozens of consulting companies through here, each telling us that they know the best way to solve our productivity and logistics problems. But every one of them only solves a small part of the problem. Are you going to come in here and give me another solution that fixes a part of our problem but leaves us missing the mark in other areas of our business? In your opinion, which solution is best?"

The author was quick to jump at the opportunity and stated, "All of them are best."

"What do you mean?" asked the general.

"You've already identified the problem," the author continued. "Each solution fixes part of your planning and scheduling problems. But none of them fixes all the problems. What I would recommend is a segmented approach. Your facility does not need a 'one size fits all' solution. It needs a segmented solution. Within each segment, a different planning and scheduling tool is optimal. We need to define the segments, select the appropriate tool for that segment, and execute using that tool. Then you will finally achieve optimality."

With that, the author and the COO proceeded to discuss the details of a segmented planning and scheduling approach for his extremely complex supply chain. That is what this book will teach the reader how to do.

First let us take a look at how good you, the reader, are at segmentation. I have included a planning and scheduling test created by Einstein. It is called the Albert Einstein Riddle. Albert Einstein wrote this riddle and claimed that if you could solve this "pure logic" problem you must be in the top 2% of the intelligent people in the world. He starts with these rules

1. On a street there are five houses painted five different colors.
2. In each house lives a person of a different nationality.

3. These five homeowners each drink a different kind of beverage, smoke different brands of cigars, and keep different pets.

The question you are trying to answer is: Who owns the fish? He offers the following clues:

1. The Brit lives in the red house.
2. The Swede keeps dogs as pets.
3. The Dane drinks tea.
4. The green house is on the left of the white house.
5. The owner of the green house drinks coffee.
6. The person who smokes Pall Mall rears birds.
7. The owner of the yellow house smokes Dunhill.
8. The man living in the center house drinks milk.
9. The Norwegian lives in the first house.
10. The man who smokes Blends lives next to the one who keeps cats.
11. The man who keeps horses lives next to the man who smokes Dunhill.
12. The man who smokes Blue Master drinks beer.
13. The German smokes Prince.
14. The Norwegian lives next to the blue house.
15. The man who smokes Blends has a neighbor who drinks water.

The answer to the riddle is found later in this book, but I won't tell you where because that would just be too easy.

Acknowledgments

In order to give credit where credit is due, I would need to create a long list of individuals, companies, universities, and countries that I have worked with. In my most recent academic past, I have had the pleasure of working with the following universities:

- University of San Diego in its Supply Chain Management Institute
- Brigham Young University
- California State University, Chico
- Numerous international universities

Professionally, I have had the pleasure of working with the following organizations:

- Wipro Consulting as a Practice Partner in Supply Chain Management
- MainStream Management as a Senior Strategy and Lean Consultant
- Infosys as a Senior Principal heading the Lean/Six Sigma/Change Management Practice
- American Management Systems (AMS) as a Senior Principal in their Corporate Technology Group
- Precision Printers as Executive Director of Quality, Engineering, R&D, Customer Service, Production Scheduling and Planning, and Facilities Management

Other organizations that I have worked for include:

- Air Force and DOD
- The State of California
- The State of Texas
- United Nations and others

I have lived and worked in factories in Latin America, Asia, and Europe. I have co-authored articles and books and have

worked with academics and professionals from as far away as
Europe, Japan, and Australia. My broad exposure to a variety
of manufacturing and service facilities all over the world has
given me the background I needed to write this book.

Introduction

Too many organizations are failing to be competitive, not because they cannot solve problems, but because they cannot identify the best solution. They haven't realized that there is not a "one size fits all" solution that will solve every problem.

Gerhard Plenert

We live in a world filled with consultants who have the perfect answer to any problem. The problem is that in order for that approach to work, every problem would have to be structurally the same. And they simply are not all the same. In this book, we address the issues of planning and scheduling and ask the question, "Is there a 'one size fits all' solution for planning and scheduling?" The answer is a resounding, "No!"
For example, historically we started with EOQ (Economic Order Quantity) as the one size fits all solution. Eventually computer power allowed us the luxury of using the more complicated MRP (Material Requirements Planning) systems. MRP allowed us to schedule materials based on work schedules or routings, but it had the flaw of assuming infinite worker capacity and therefore was plagued with scheduling shortages. Next, we had JIT (Just In Time), which focused on optimizing the scheduling of materials movement. This was followed by TOC (Theory of Constraints), which optimized machine bottlenecks. Each of these systems looked at the facility as if it had one focused problem: optimizing work schedules, optimizing materials movement, or optimizing machine utilization. But what if you have two, or possibly even all three of these problems? Then what system do you use? Or what if your critical resource is not labor, materials, or machinery? What if it is energy, as in the case of aluminum, or logistics as in the case of apparel or bottling? Then which planning and scheduling solution do you utilize?

This book introduces the concept of segmentation as the planning and scheduling tool that facilitates the optimization of the supply chain. If you have one type of problem in a part of your supply chain, you use the solution that appropriately focuses on that problem. If you have a different problem in a different part of your supply chain, then you use a different and appropriate tool for that part of the supply chain, and so forth.

That is what segmentation does. It applies the appropriate tool to the appropriate part of the supply chain. It breaks us free from "one size fits all" thinking.

The purpose of this book is to provide private companies and government agencies with the tools to:

- Understand the power of segmentation
- Develop a systematic plan for the implementation of segmentation in the supply chain
- Understand the components of an integrated segmentation policy
- Understand the analytics elements of Supply Chain Segmentation (SCS)
- Understand the measures that define segmentation success
- Develop a strategy and methodology to introduce segmentation principles

The book will discuss how to integrate planning and scheduling tools using a segmentation approach resulting in a world-class environment. This book will provide professional, objective, and valuable information to solve many of the major planning and scheduling challenges. It will demonstrate solutions to these challenges by using stories and examples of how segmentation management improvements have successfully made a difference in both the private and government sectors. To do this, the book will give detailed examples of several organizations that solved different problems using a segmented planning and scheduling structure.

Let us now move forward and see how segmentation, when augmented by analytics and when applied to the supply chain, can have a dramatic effect on the performance of your organization.

SECTION 1

Segmentation

1

What Is Segmentation and How Does It Work?

If you want to live a happy life,
Tie it to a Goal.

Albert Einstein

What Is Segmentation?

Segmentation is about differentiating. As we can see in Chart 1.1, there are differences. Segmentation is about realizing that not all customers and products are the same. At the same time, there are still some common characteristics that allow a certain level of process standardization. In the rare case where we have one product with one supplier and one

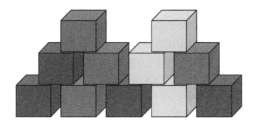

Chart 1.1 Without Segmentation

customer, segmentation is meaningless. But as soon as we add a second customer to the mix, we find that the two customers expect to be supported differently. The difference could be a location difference, where one is further away than the other is. Or, it could be a timing difference, where the delivery to one customer is more critical than the other. Or, possibly a quality requirement difference. Or, it could be a personality difference making us more compatible with one customer than the other. And the potential differences go on and on. The result is that we manage our two customers differently. We treat them differently. We respond differently to their requests.

Now let us grow our business to where we have dozens of customers. Some customers buy more than others do and therefore they become a preferred customer. Some customers complain more, and therefore get more attention. And the list of differentiators goes on and on. In the end, we treat customers differently.

Now let us grow our customer base to hundreds or even thousands of customers. Suddenly our customers lose their individuality. We still respond to the complainers differently than the non-complainers, and we respond to the large customers differently. But, our customers start losing their individual identity. They start becoming a number that is part of a list or group of customers of one type or another. In the belief that we are increasing our efficiency and that we are setting a policy of treating our customers fairly, we start treating all customers the same. We implement policies, systems, and procedures that become rigid in an attempt to be consistent. We believe consistency generates efficiency and stability through standardization. This is true, but there is an even better way to manage these customers and still take advantage of the ability to standardize.

Becoming even more realistic, we next complicate our organization even more by increasing the number of products produced, and then by increasing the number of suppliers that provide input into the process. We can quickly see how the complexity of this process can become overwhelming. Let us look at a real-life example of exactly what I am describing.

Mail-Order Pharmacy

In the pharmaceutical industry, we have both neighbor-hood pharmacies and mail-order pharmacies. In one specific example of a rather large mail-order pharmacy, we find that this organization has grown so fast that it no longer distinguishes between the various types of customers that it has. Its customers include hospitals, clinics, and individual households or patients. However, the pharmacy no longer knows which prescription deliveries are critical and which ones are not. The result is that the lack of information and customer differentiation has forced this pharmacy to treat all prescription deliveries as critical. They overnight ship all prescriptions, regardless of their importance. Often the shipment is not critical because the customer may have an existing supply on hand, but again, the pharmacy has lost the ability to track individual information. It has never created any way of identifying or distinguishing the difference in its customers. And the result is that its shipping costs have become enormous.

If you look at this example, in the way I presented it, the solution becomes obvious. However, the pharmacy that I am describing was so caught up in growth and in customer service, that it never took the time to step back and say, "This doesn't make sense. There must be a better way." It was too busy fighting fires to realize how much money it was losing on shipping costs. It felt that customer service was the most important. But it didn't realize that through a segmented approach it could not only reduce shipping cost, but also simultaneously increase customer service.

Let us take a closer look at the pharmacy's process. The pharmacy purchases drugs from suppliers all over the world. Depending on the supplier, some level of certification and testing is required. All of this occurs before the drugs arrive at the pharmacy. However, all of these steps have an impact on delivery time. Once they have arrived, the drugs are placed into bins. But, there is an added complication. This pharmacy not only manages the drugs for itself, but also provides a drug distribution service for other pharmacies. So, the drugs of any one specific type may be deposited into the bins of any one of the three companies that it services. Therefore, pills ABC arrive at the pharmacy for distribution under company X and are placed in the ABC bin for company X. Similarly, ABC also arrives for company Y and is in turn stored in the ABC bin for company Y.

Fortunately, the pill picking process is automated. As long as the pills are put into the correct bins, the prescription bottles are filled and labeled with the appropriate pills, given the appropriate pharmacy name and label, and sent down the line for shipping. At the shipping location, the pill bottles are put in an envelope and labeled for shipping. However, at this point another complication may occur. What if the same patient is getting multiple prescriptions? Wouldn't it make sense to ship all these together and consolidate the shipping costs? Sometimes that happens, but often it does not.

Let us complicate the process even more. What if we have multiple patients at the same hospital, each getting his or her own prescription filled? Currently, the hospital receives multiple shipments, one for each patient. This becomes expensive in shipping costs for the pharmacy, and it is a nuisance for the hospital because it needs to open several shipping envelopes when all the different orders could have come together as one shipment. Moreover, wouldn't it be more convenient if somehow the critical or urgent shipments were identified differently than the ones that were not as urgent? Right now, the pharmacy and the hospital are forced to treat all shipments as urgent because there is no way to distinguish the difference.

So what would segmentation do differently in this example? How would it help? The first and most important step in segmentation is the identification of the goal. What are we trying to accomplish? Are we trying to reduce shipping cost? Are we trying to improve customer service by putting more focus on the urgent shipments and less importance on the non-urgent shipments? Are we trying to reduce inventory by improving the planning process? Knowing what it is that we are trying to accomplish shifts our priorities and therefore changes the criteria used in segmentation, as we will see in later chapters.

Let us continue with our pharmacy example. In this case, the goal is customer service—"getting the right product to the correct customer on time." If that was its only goal, then what it is doing now—shipping everything overnight express—is good enough because it achieves that goal. The pharmacy should just go ahead and overnight FedEx everything to its customers. It gets the pharmacy what it needs when it needs it. Unfortunately, it may go bankrupt in the process, so there has to be a secondary goal, which in this case is "being competitive."

Defining what it means to be competitive requires not just revenue and profit, but also requires us to look at what would differentiate our service from our competitors' service. In the pharmacy example, the organization is a mail-order pharmacy. It does not have the convenience of just being in a retail outlet down the street where its customers can stop in and quickly pick up their pills. So what differentiates this organization? The key benefit it offers is that it can provide the drugs to your door without you having to leave the house. This becomes important for patients who have disabilities, or who are getting older in years thereby making a trip to the local pharmacy challenging. Therefore, the mail-order pharmacy needs to get the drugs to the customer as quickly as possible and have them delivered to the patient's door so the patient does not have to venture out of the house.

The mail-order process is also convenient for hospitals and clinics. They don't have to stock up on all drugs. They can have the correct prescription delivered through the mail system ahead of when the patient needs them.

Let us get back to the concept of segmentation. How would it help our mail-order pharmacy? It turns out that there are several different specific areas where segmentation can simultaneously reduce cost and improve customer service. Segmentation can provide a basis for the following:

1. Differentiating urgent from non-urgent deliveries based on the product being delivered. For example, refrigerated products require overnight turn-around. Alternatively, prescriptions that are renewals are not as urgent as new prescriptions.
2. Customers can be segmented by type. For example, hospitals tend to have more urgent needs than a clinic because hospitals handle emergencies whereas clinics handle

more repetitive customers. In the case of clinics, they tend to distribute the medicine when the patient comes in for treatment, and the schedules are fixed and regular.
3. Receipt of drugs can be managed by priority. For example, is this particular drug running low on supply at this customer location?

At this point, we have discussed some of the reasoning behind segmentation, but we have kept our example extremely simplistic. Identification of the best and most meaningful segmentation structure requires analytics and data analysis. For example, factors like service level, demand variability, forecast reliability, inventory stocking rules, shelf life, etc., all come into play when creating the optimal segmentation structure. We will see how all of this works in the next chapters.

Moving away from our example, let us look at retail segmentation. Segmentation for a retail organization or a distributor would focus on the customer. It would have only one set of SKUs. The same SKU numbers that are used on the procurement side are also used on the delivery side. That makes the segmentation criteria different then in manufacturing. In manufacturing you typically have an entirely different set of SKUs for the procurement side (or supply side) than you do for the delivery side (or demand side) of the process. In this case, two entirely different segmentation exercises are often required. The process will be explained in more detail in future chapters, but for now I just want to increase your awareness that segmentation is not executed the same way for all organizations and for all processes.

Aircraft Engine Manufacturer

Let us look at a second real-life example. In this case, we are looking at an aircraft engine manufacturing facility. This organization has hundreds of suppliers from all over the world shipping materials through a series of warehouses. Initially the materials are staged and consolidated in an overseas warehouse. Then they are shipped to a redistribution ware-house in the United States from which they are fed into the production facility as required by the manufacturing process. After production, the finished goods, which are manufactured aircraft parts, are again staged at an out-going warehouse and sent on to Boeing, Airbus, or any of their other competitors.

As you can see in this aircraft engine manufacturing example, there are two major groups of SKUs. The Supply side SKUs and the Demand side SKUs. For the Supply side, segmentation would be used to help manage the planning, scheduling, consolidation, and cost reduction of the incoming materials through the supply chain. For the Demand side, segmentation would focus on customer responsiveness and finished goods inventory minimization. You have two different segmentation structures with two different sets of goals. The Demand side planners would have a very different job from the Supply side planners, and their optimization tools would look different as well.

With this background, I think it is time for a textbook defi-nition of segmentation given from my perspective:

> **Segmentation** is an organizational strategy tool that involves dividing a target set of resources (like customers, products, sup-pliers, locations, etc.) into subsets where each subset has common characteristics or common needs. Each segment is optimized by customizing planning and scheduling tools to maximize the goals of that segment, which could include customer satisfaction, on-time delivery, inventory optimization, cost minimization, etc.

While there may theoretically be "ideal" segment struc-tures, in reality every organization engaged in segmentation will develop different ways of organizing their segments based on a different set of priorities or goals. They will create dif-ferentiation strategies to exploit each segment. Successful seg-mentation and a corresponding product strategy can give a firm a commercial advantage, due to the more effective match between the target customer and the product. As demonstrated in Chart 1.2, segmentation can be the differentiator that takes advantage of your organization's uniqueness and makes you a market leader.

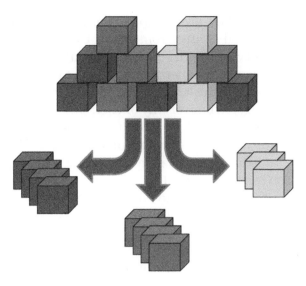

Chart 1.2 Types of Segmentation

Retail Segmentation

The roots of segmentation come out of the retail industry. Retailing was the first to recognize the advantages that segmentation brings to the table. For historical purposes, we should look at the lessons learned by retailing as we expand these concepts into Supply Chain Segmentation (SCS). Retail Market Segmentation presents us with an excellent case example of how segmentation has helped. The earlier definition of segmentation fits well for Retail Market Segmentation.

As we explore some of the relevant lessons learned in Retail Market Segmentation, we are taught that segmentation follows several specific structural groupings (see Chart 1.3). The use of these groupings is what allows us to customize the segmentation structure and therefore makes it more powerful. The groupings used in Retail Market Segmentation are:

Geographic segmentation (Where?)—Here, the market is segmented according to geographic criteria, for example by nation, state, region, county, city, or even down to neighborhood or zip codes. The geo-cluster

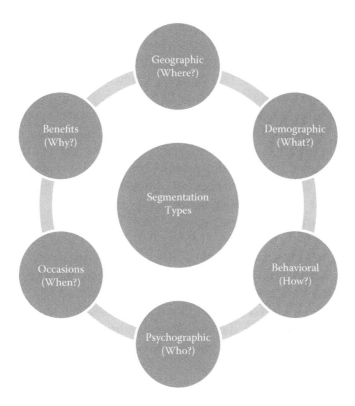

Chart 1.3 The Critical Resources of a Supply Chain

segmentation approach combines demographic data with geographic data to create a more accurate profile of the specific characteristics of that local. For example, in rainy regions you sell raincoats, umbrellas, and boots. In hot regions, you sell summer wear. In cold regions, you sell warm clothes.

Psychographic segmentation (Who?)—Psychographics is the science of using psychology and demographics to better understand consumer expectations. In psychographic segmentation, consumers are divided according to their lifestyle, personality, values, and social class. Consumers within the same geographic group can exhibit very different psychographic profiles.

Positive market segmentation (What?)—Here, we do market segmenting by dividing the market into groups of individual markets with similar wants or needs.

The company divides its markets into distinct groups, which have distinct needs, wants, and behaviors. These customers might want different products and services. Broadly, markets can be divided according to a number of general criteria, such as by industry or public versus private. This part of the segmentation process consists of drawing up a perceptual map that highlights rival goods within one's industry according to customer perceived quality and price. The map allows the firm to consider the marketing communications mix best suited to the product in question.

Behavioral segmentation (How?)—Consumers are divided into groups according to their knowledge of, attitude toward, use of, or response to a product.

Occasions (When?)—In this category, segmentation is based on occasions such as the arising of a special need and desire in consumers at various occasions. For example, products specific to a certain holiday like Christmas or Diwali. Another type of occasional market segment includes people preparing for weddings or funerals.

Benefits (Why?)—Segmentation can take place based on the benefits sought by the consumer, or based on the benefits that the product or service can provide.

Moving forward with the Retail Segmentation example, let us look at how Retail Market Segmentation uses this segmentation tool. The following are some examples.

Customer retention—The basic approach to customer retention-based segmentation is that a company tags each of its active customers with three values:

1. Is this customer at risk of canceling the company's service? The most common indicator of high-risk customers is a drop off in the usage of the company's service.
2. Is this customer worth retaining? This boils down to whether the post-retention profit from the customer is expected to be more than the cost to retain the customer.

3. What retention tactics should be used? If the customer is deemed worthy of saving, then the company needs to know which save tactics are most likely to be successful. Tactics commonly used include providing special customer discounts or sending customers communications that reinforce the value of the given service.

Niche marketing—A niche is a customer group that seeks a distinct set of benefits or has a unique set of needs, which requires specialization. This often attracts a smaller group of competitors.

Local marketing—Marketing programs tailored to the needs of a localized customer group.

Price discrimination—When a monopoly exists, the price of a product is likely to be higher than in a competitive market. These profits can be increased further if the market can be segmented with different prices charged to different segments allowing the company to charge higher prices to those segments willing and able to pay more.

Analytics

In any segmentation approach, there is an analytics piece. Once we have defined the type of segmentation we want to use, we then need to specify the criteria, segmentation model, and corresponding calculations that will be necessary to execute and define which customer belongs to which segment. Various algorithms and approaches are defined. For instance, customers might be segmented by gender (male or female), attitudes (progressive or conservative), age (<30 or ≥30), or income ($<$US $300,000) vs. $\geq$US $300,000). A segmentation model is developed and each customer is evaluated using this model. From this, they are broken out into their individual segments.

Retail Market Segmentations can be obtained by any number of analytics approaches. Simplistically, an existing discrete variable may be chosen to define the segments. But more often, segmentation requires an analytics research project to collect data on numerous attributes and then uses statistical analyses tools to identify which sets of attributes offer the clearest definition of the customer. Using this we can then define the segments. This process is often called "post-hoc" segmentation. Common statistical techniques for segmentation analysis include clustering algorithms such as K-means or Cluster Analysis. Often the analytics process uses statistical mixture models such as Latent Class Analysis or it uses ensemble approaches such as Random Forests.

Once the segmentation structure has been defined and the segments are planned, the company's behavior toward each of the segments needs to be mapped out. How will each of the segments be treated differently? A separate and specific marketing strategy needs to be defined for each of the segments. What will the customer service level be for each segment? What is an acceptable lead time for response? What is our tolerance of cost overruns or losses with each segment? And so on.

Supply Chain Segmentation (SCS)

Returning to the topic of this book, Supply Chain Segmentation, we use the Retail Market Segmentation structure as a foundation for developing a segmentation approach that fits Supply Chains recognizing the increased complexities that we will encounter. As outlined earlier in this chapter, Supply Chains have distinctly different Demand side and Supply side requirements. The result is that their segmentation structure is also very different in each.

In the next chapter, we will explore some of the characteristics of a Supply Chain. Then, in the following chapters, we will go into detail about how SCS works and we will offer a few examples of its application. We will also spend some time describing the SCS analytics process including an explanation of some of the tools that can be utilized. We start by pressing forward with a definition of world of the Supply Chain.

Be a yardstick of quality. Some people aren't used to an environment where excellence is expected.

Steve Jobs

References

Goldstein, Doug. "What is Customer Segmentation?" http://www.mindofmarketing.net/2007/05/customer-segmentation-why-exactly-does.html#.UlNInU3D-lg. May 2007.

Gupta, Sunil, and Donald R. Lehmann. Customer-based strategy. In: *Managing Customers as Investments: The Strategic Value of Customers in the Long Run*. Upper Saddle River, NJ: Pearson Education/Wharton School Publishing, 2005, pp. 70–77.

Kotler, Philip, and Kevin Lane Keller. What is geographic segmentation? In: *Marketing Management*, 12th ed. Englewood Cliffs, NJ: Prentice Hall, 2006.

Sheth-Voss, Pieter, and Ismael Carreras. How informative is your segmentation? A simple new metric yields surprising results, *Marketing Research*, pp. 8–13, Winter 2010, American Marketing Association.

2

The Supply Chain*

Here at HP, 65 cents of every revenue dollar is consumed by the Supply Chain. Supply Chain has a direct impact on customer perception, brand perception, and customer satisfaction. Supply Chain is ultimately responsible for the price of the products, product quality, lead times, and predictability. So it has a direct, I mean absolutely direct, impact on the customer, on the stock valuation, and on shareholder value.

Dick Conrad, Hewlett-Packard's Senior Vice President,
Global Operations Supply Chain[†]

Defining the Supply Chain

When defining a Supply Chain, you will encounter terms such as:

Sourcing
Integrating
Connectivity
Information Exchange
Communication
Linkages
Logistics

---

[*] Some sections of this chapter were pulled from the books *Reinventing Lean: Introducing Lean Management Into the Supply Chain*, Elsevier Science, 2007, and *International Operations Management*, Copenhagen Business School Press, Copenhagen, Denmark, 2002, reprinted in India by Ane Books, New Delhi, 2003. These books offer an extensive expansion of these fundamental SCM concepts. Included by permission from the author Gerhard Plenert.

[†] Terry, Lisa. Adapt or die, *CSCO*, August, 2005, p. 25.

All of these terms are appropriate in describing a Supply Chain. However, they are too generic and too broad to supply a meaningful definition to someone who does not already understand what a Supply Chain is. For the purposes of this book, we will start with a one-word definition of a Supply Chain and then we will build on it to create understanding. That one word is "Movement." Supply Chains are all about moving things around. Then, building on this one-word definition we need to decide what movements we need to track. And the answer is, "We need to track the movement of resources."

Which leads to the next question, "What resources are moved in a Supply Chain?" Obviously, when we initially think of a Supply Chain we think of materials or parts moving from one location to another and eventually ending up in the hands of a customer. For example, when we think of the Supply Chain for a television, we start at the mine that digs up the raw materials, then it goes to the refinery where the steel or the chemicals are processed, and then it moves to the factory where parts are formed and assembled, which eventually become the components, the circuit boards, or screens. Finally, the parts arrive at the assembly plant, which results in the final product of a television. The television moves to the shipping company where it is packaged and delivered, then on to a warehouse, and then to a retailer. The retail store puts the television on the shelf where the customer selects the product, purchases it, and takes it home. There are literally thousands of steps in this process. Each of these steps becomes critical to the success of the overall Supply Chain. Ultimately, the customer interprets a failure in any of these steps as a failure of the entire Supply Chain.

As complex as the Supply Chain seems from a materials flow perspective, we soon realize that this is not the complete Supply Chain. There is more than the flow of materials that ultimately defines a Supply Chain's success or failure. There are two other critical resources whose movement defines Supply Chain success. These other resources include information and money. Just as with materials, a failure in the flow of either of these other two resources is a failure of the entire Supply Chain. And in the end, the customer's perspective is the only perspective that counts.

For example, in the movement of money, failure in processing a payment, charging the wrong amount, or collecting the
incorrect amount is a failure in the Supply Chain. Looking at
the information movement side, failure to process the order
correctly, supplying an incorrect product definition or shipment date or an incorrect materials list, etc., can result in a
delay in the completion of the process or, worse yet, an incorrect product being shipped to a customer.

The result is that there are at least three critical resources
that define the success or failure of all the "movements" within
the Supply Chain. Any one of these resources is no more or
less important than are any of the others. A failure of any is
a failure of all. The result is shown in the model in Chart 2.1.

In Chart 2.1, we see the three critical "moving" resources.
It also shows an area of overlap and interaction for the three
resources. None of these resources exists in isolation and a
change to any one of the three often affects the performance of
one or both of the other resources.

Looking at Chart 2.1 it is easy to conclude that in optimizing
the Supply Chain and thereby making our Supply Chain world
class, all we need to do is optimize these three movements. This
is only partially true. Once again, the model in Chart 2.1 is
far too simplistic to explain everything that goes on within a
Supply Chain. When optimizing the movement of these three
resources, we also need to look at the forces that interact with
them. This list of forces can become quite long and complex.
For example, time pressures like holidays or work schedules
can affect the performance of the Supply Chain. Alternatively,
technology availability and change can affect the performance

The Critical Resources That Define a Supply Chain

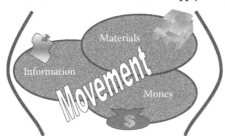

Chart 2.1 The Critical Resources of a Supply Chain

The Forces Affecting The Resources That Define a Supply Chain

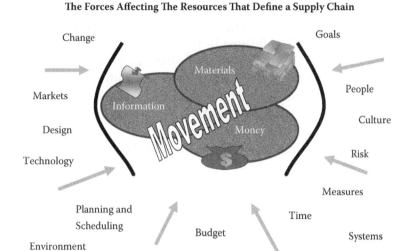

Chart 2.2 The Forces Affecting the Supply Chain

of the Supply Chain. A graphic representation of some of these forces or pressures can be seen in Chart 2.2.

From Chart 2.2 we see pressures like risk, time, and budgets that need to become part of the optimization process of any Supply Chain. For example, timeliness can be prohibitively expensive and therefore impractical. Therefore, the balancing act of all these resources and pressures, optimized in conjunction with each other will optimize the total Supply Chain. Before we dig deeper into identifying the perfect Supply Chain, let us take a short look at some of the history surrounding the development of Supply Chains.

A Little History

When looking at the migration of Supply Chain productivity, quality, and delivery performance over time, we find that this migration was often driven by two key factors:

1. The capabilities of the available technology
2. The availability and cost of resources

For example, in the 1970s and earlier, the focus was on labor efficiency. Organizations were internally focused. During this period, labor was still the resource that dominated the highest concentration of cost content for most types of manufacturing. The belief persisted that if people worked more efficiently and harder, they would generate more output. The production planning systems during that era would support labor-based strategies. These systems migrated from EOQ (Economic Order Quantity, which based all control on inventory levels) to MRP (Material Requirements Planning, which introduced the scheduling of labor, materials, and machinery) to MRP II (Manufacturing Resources Planning, bringing financial and marketing considerations into the production planning process) to ERP (Enterprise Resources Planning, which integrated all the information systems in an organization and looked at the enterprise, not just the manufacturing plant). Similarly for distribution, we have DRP (Distribution Requirements Planning). The traditional focus was always internal, looking for improvements within the organization.

The 1980s blossomed with a fascination for substitute production planning philosophies like JIT (Just in Time) from Japan or TOC (Theory of Constraints—initially called OPT or Optimized Production Technology) from Israel. These systems shifted the focus away from labor toward materials and machine efficiency. However, the direction of the focus was still internal. Moreover, these new systems were simply adopted under the ERP planning wing, and treated as subsets of the ERP planning and scheduling environment.

At this point, organizations were obsessed with the fear of sharing too much information. As such, vendors and customers were "black boxes" where no information exchange was allowed. However, as we moved into the 1990s organizations started to recognize the influence of external factors in overall profitability. Companies identified how customers, vendors, and partners played key roles in the performance of their overall Supply Chain. Organizations began to acknowledge how working with customers and vendors, and sharing information with these "outsiders" was critical in defining not just the external performance of the Supply Chain, but also the internal performance of the organization.

As significant as this new external Supply Chain perspective was, it unfortunately did not create harmony between the Supply Chain partners. Rather, a jockeying for power occurred, where a financial kingpin in the Supply Chain would attempt to control the entire Supply Chain. At times, we find that the manufacturer tries to control and drive the performance of the Supply Chain, as in the case of General Motors or Ford. At other times, we find that the retailer controls the Supply Chain, as in the case of Walmart.

Breaking into the 2000s, we find organizations that realize that customers and vendors are not stupid and that they can contribute value to the Supply Chain. Working with customers and vendors as Supply Chain partners, and using their input rather than just dictating to them what is expected, brings an entirely new perspective into the management and control of the overall process. This introduced the idea of a value chain. Now each participant in the process adds value to and receives value from the overall Supply Chain and its partners. The value chain (end-to-end Supply Chain) has been created and relationships are no longer fixed, controlled, and rigid. Suppliers can be interchanged based on the availability of resources within any of the vendors.

Using Dell Computers as an example during this time, let me give you an approach for a fully integrated, end-to-end e-commerce based Supply Chain (eVCM or e-commerce value chain). In their purchasing process, customers would go online and would identify and create the customized configuration of the product they wanted to purchase. For example, if they wanted a laptop computer, they would configure the computer exactly the way they wanted it to look. Then, the online system would give them the pricing of their selected configuration. Everything we have described, up to this point, already exists. The next step would then be to blow this configuration out throughout the Supply Chain, to check product availability down to the vendor's vendor level. This is referred to as Available to Promise (ATP) validation. If there were no product availability, then the system would check for capacity availability. This is referred to as Capable to Promise (CTP) validation. These systems require a high degree of information collaboration all the way up and down the Supply Chain. Using information collaboration, the eVCM system would then allocate product and capacity for manufacturing and shipping at all levels in the Supply Chain and come back to the customers (while they are still online) and give them a precise delivery date (currently the system only offers the customer an approximate delivery date, which includes a significant buffer).

If the customer moves forward with the order by paying for the order, then all the inventory and capacity allocations become firm and the production and delivery process for the laptop computer is triggered. From this example, we can see a movement of the three critical resources in a Supply Chain:

Materials
Money
Information

We can see how an error in managing any one of these resources is a failure of the entire system. For example, if inventory records were incorrect, then the production, shipping, and delivery schedules would be incorrect. Or if the cost or payment calculations are incorrect, then the profitability of the entire supply chain is affected. The performance of all three resources is interconnected, as are the forces that put pressure on these resources, like time, planning and scheduling, or the systems used to make the eVCM work.

Looking into the future, we see international marketplaces for resources. Labor was cheapest in Mexico, then in India, then in China and some of the old Soviet Bloc countries. Similarly, information processing through Internet-based resources can be processed anywhere in the world. We find manufacturers moving to tax-free zones or production areas with fewer restrictions and regulations. In addition, the same is true with money, which can now be managed in a variety of locations all over the world. Supply Chains are becoming increasingly complex and the supply network that is the most efficient, and not the manufacturer that is the most efficient, will dominate market share.

What Is Supply Chain Management (SCM)?

The purpose of a management process is to maximize the performance and the success of the process. We have had Supply Chain processes since the first time there was an exchange of goods. The hunter exchanged skins for the farmer's crops. That introduced the Supply Chain. At some later point, the intermediary arrived. They incorporated a delivery system into the Supply Chain, someone who would bring the crops from the farmer to the hunter, and vice versa. Then the market sprang up where goods were traded at a central location. And so on until we arrive at the incredibly complex Supply Chains that we see today.

Supply Chain Management (SCM) is about goal setting. There are numerous ways to address the identification of goals. One technique is by identifying what a world class Supply Chain environment would look like. This process can be accomplished using two tools:

Benchmarking
Step Charting

In benchmarking, we start by going out into the literature (books, journal and magazine articles, conference proceedings, website postings, etc.) to identify what the "best practices" are as related to SCM for your particular industry. Once you have created a list of best practices, these are now categorized into the four classifications of a step chart. Chart 2.3 is an example of an SCM step chart. It is not intended to be all-inclusive, nor will it fit your specific industry. Additionally, step charts are date stamped so that what is world class today will not be world class one year from now. However, we can use Chart 2.3 as an example of what a step chart should look like.

From Chart 2.3 we see four categories of classification. Each of the categories identifies a different type of organization. They are as follows:

- Clerical—The clerical organization is one that operates in a foundational mode. It is dictatorial, top-down directed, and has a militaristic style. It generally

World Class SCM

Clerical (1–3)	Mechanical (4–5)	Proactive (6–8)	World Class (9–10)
Goal: Bottom-line impact	Goal: Bottom line Impact – Revenue	Goal: Bottom line impact	Goal: Company wide goals and initiatives
Focus: Inward	Focus: Inward, putting out fires, react to complaints	Focus: Fulfill social responsibility, customer focus	Focus: Total cost of ownership (TCO)
Data: Historical and Minimal	Emphasis: Purchase price, cost and budget conscious	Strategy: Reduce non-value added	Strategy: Strategic planning
Metrics: Minimal and Transactional	Data: Minimal data interface, on request, batch reporting	Emphasis: Cost, Quality, timeliness; bottom line, revenue driven	Emphasis: Performance to customer & shareholder expectations
Systems/Technology: No Automated Production Planning System	Reporting: Low level	Data: Central repository	Data: Utilized for strategic planning
Staffing: Minimal training/No cross training/no teaming/no reward system	Metrics: Focused on function and transaction activity	Reporting: Reduce forecasting errors, high level reporting	Reporting: Regular reporting to the executives, customers, and vendors
Management: Top Down, Reactive	Systems/Technology: Computers process paperwork	Metrics: Focused on company goals, but not integrated or cross-functional, departmental focus	Metrics: Extensive lean and change focused metrics
Process: Manual paperwork based process, redundant, highly transactional	Relationships: Transactional/Adversarial	Systems/Technology: Requirements planning systems	Systems/Technology: Lean and Cycle Time Reduction Initiatives
Change: Lack of foresight/no linkage to continuous improvement/strong resistance	Staffing: Cross training minimal, employee recognition systems	Relationships: Transactional and collaborative	Relationships: Collaborative cross functional teams involving both customers and suppliers
Work Environment: Silos	Management: Top down with fewer layers	Staffing: Development of cross-functional teams	Staffing: Extensive training programs
Inventory: Poorly planned – too much in some areas and too little in others	Vendor/Customer Relationships: Minimal and sporadic	Management: Participative Management considered	Management: Participative/Empowered teams
	Quality: Measure and address problems as they arise	Vendor/Customer Relationships: Focus on improving customer satisfaction	Vendor/Customer Relationships: Strategic Sourcing; Customer Focus
	Change: No continuous process improvement program in place	Process: Integrated to pull materials and minimize transactions	Process: Integrated to pull material, minimize transactions
	Work Environment: Silos	Quality: Focus on defect free materials	Quality: Near zero defects internal and external
	Supply Chain Management: React to requisitions	Change: Internal Continuous Process Improvement Program in Place	Change: Lean, TQM, Change Management Systems
	Inventory: Overhauling of material, minimal inventory management	Work Environment: Automation, e-Commerce	Work Environment: Pull based Lean/TOC/JIT/Kanbans/QFD (Quality Functional Deployment)
		Supply Chain Management: Perceived as adding value; involved in strategy development	Supply Chain Management: Integrated Supply Chain and Logistics systems
		Inventory: Point of use supermarkets	Inventory: Inventory levels minimized

| 1 | 2 | 3 | 4 | 5 | 6 | 7 | 8 | 9 | 10 |

Chart 2.3 World Class SCM

contains some type of dominant authority figure. This organization is generally a manual operation that is non-receptive to leading edge concepts and opposes change.

- Mechanical—The mechanical organization has recognized the need to introduce some minimal level of technology. This organization is still missing integration and organization-wide direction. The focus of the organization is departmentalized and the focus is on the performance of the individual department. Communication beyond the organization to the customer or the vendor is minimal.

- Proactive—The proactive organization is one that feels the need for integration within the organization. Company goals are established and the various departments attempt to align themselves with these goals. There is some recognition of the need to interface with vendors and customers, but these relationships are still at arm's length. Some teaming exists. Quality optimization and some levels of automation are being introduced.

- World class—This is the ideal, perfect world for your industry. It contains a high level of integration within the organization and external to the organization with customers and vendors. It contains automation and leading edge, sophisticated management, planning, and scheduling systems. Appropriate, goal-based metrics and the supportive data collection systems exist. Change is a goal and has become a natural part of the organization.

Looking at Chart 2.3, we are now ready to rank the current state of our organization. The hard part is being honest with ourselves. The tendency is to over-rank ourselves. Simply because one of our 10 departments has MRP does not mean that we are proactive. We need to look at our organization as an outsider would and realistically evaluate our performance. If, for example, we have some, but less than half of the characteristics of a mechanical environment generally applied throughout our organization, then we should not be ranked more than a 4. If we have about half, we would probably rate about a 4.5. We would use similar rankings for all categories of organizations. This gives us our "current state ranking."

Again, looking at Chart 2.3 we should now look at where our organization is heading. Again, we must be careful to be meaningful. We don't want to know where you personally think the organization is heading. We want to know where the rhetoric and the actions of the leadership of the organization seem to be guiding us. Again, we want to rank carefully and realistically the future state of the organization on a scale of 1 to 10. This assessment will give us the "future state" ranking.[*]

At this point, you have an example of what an SCM step chart should look like. You still need to customize the step chart for your organization. I have included an example of the customization of this step chart for the logistics operation of a large manufacturer (Chart 2.4). From this example, you should be able to better understand what is expected in order for you to develop your own organization-specific step chart.

At this point, you should have:

1. Customized the step chart to fit your organization.
2. Identified your "current state" ranking on the step chart.
3. Identified your "future state" ranking on the step chart, which now becomes the goal of your organization.

You are now ready to move forward in developing a strategy for implementation. However, before we look at the section on strategy, let us consider some optional Supply Chain Models.

A Model

We will now look at a couple of SCM models, which may or may not fit your organization but which can help you visualize your SCM structure. The purpose of considering optional/alterna-

---

[*] A more detailed discussion about step chart rankings and how to create a customized step chart can be found in the book *Reinventing Lean: Introducing Lean Management Into the Supply Chain*, Elsevier Science, 2007.

World Class Logistics

Clerical			Mechanical		Proactive			World Class	
No Logistics Strategy Telephone Fax Email Partial Electronic P.O. Development Partial Electronic RFQ Generation Purchasing Cards Company Centric Focus Data Not Readily Available Spot Purchasing on Web Web Used as Search Tool for New Suppliers No Electronic Enabled Collaboration Islands of Information			Transaction Focus Web Based Forms Electronic P.O. Development (MRP or Other System) Electronic RFQ/RFP Generation Electronic Procurement of MRO & Selected Indirect Materials Open Loop SRM Systems Intranet Disperses Information Price Focused Reverse Auctions Electronically Enabled Internal Order Transfers Identify New Suppliers Performance Reviews of Suppliers - Inventory Tracking Systems Kaizen events create temporary improvements in supplier quality Forecasts are Shared Little or No Training is Available for logistics Electronic Supplier Performance Rating System Data is Internally Focused		Potential causes of quality failures are identified & eliminated Electronic integration of P.O. ; JIT, MRP and TOC Systems Environmental issues related are addressed in design Fail-safe systems are implemented Internal suggestion system activated Safety is addressed in design A quality management training program is implemented Goals set are achievable & based on facts, not stretch percentages Supplier process capability is measured against design tolerances Utilizes SPC for preventing failures Robust quality with reduced variance Utilizes design of experiments Utilizes value engineering Tandem use of discontinuous & continuous improvement Concurrent engineering occurs in product & service design Activities that drive quality costs are linked to improvement processes Supplier alliances aid in total quality cost reduction Supplier certification utilized Quality management is the responsibility of everyone in the firm Process improvement is championed by the power bearer in the process			Seamless Communications via Cross Supply Chain Seamless integration of the electronic P.O. Development using JIT, MRP, and TOC System Environmental issues related to quality are addressed in design Implement environmental methodologies, project timeline, and resource needs, goals, and objectives Electronic Catalogs Include Strategic Data & Design Information Designs are Created Electronically with Key Suppliers Electronic Generation of Contracts All Payments are Electronic Data integration system/tools used throughout the supply chain (i.e. RFID) Training includes chain members Contingency plans developed collaboratively by chain members for disasters, strikes & acts of nature Collaborative Design Including Suppliers Occurs in Real Time Supply Chain Collaboration Hubs Firewalls allow collaborative data transfer while still protecting critical information Cost information used to continuously improve supply chain processes Design processes interlinked with supply chain Fully linked e-commerce with suppliers, databases & systems Fully linked cost databases & systems TCO measured across chain	
1	2	3	4	5	6	7	8	9	10

Chart 2.4 World Class Logistics

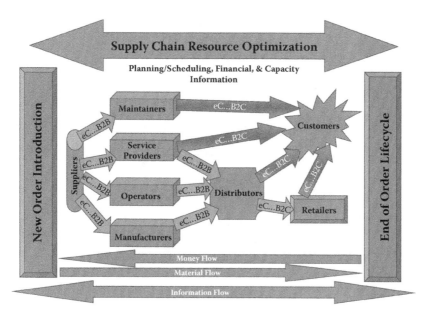

Chart 2.5 Supply Chain Resource Model

tive models is to facilitate your thought process as you attempt to define your SCM step chart.

A model that is focused on the flow and the optimization of the Supply Chain can be seen in Chart 2.5. In this model, we look at the materials, money, and information flow that occur in a Supply Chain. We look at all the steps that occur in this process and that move the product from its inception (new order introduction) through to its completion (end of order lifecycle) and delivery to the customer.

Another example of a Supply Chain model can be seen in Chart 2.6. This model keys in on the planning process that occurs within the supply network. It shows how the process is cyclical and integrated. The process starts with Demand Planning, which is triggered by forecasts and customer orders. The long-term planning process becomes a short-term supply scheduling process where materials, information, and money are initially scheduled and then moved through the process starting with the supplier, through to the producer, and on to the finished product. The third stage of the process is Demand Fulfillment, where the delivery system kicks in and the customer product is delivered.

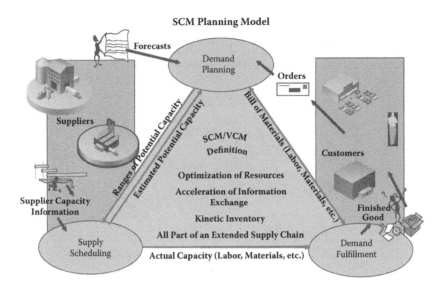

Chart 2.6 Supply Chain Planning Model

Each of the models has a story to tell about the Supply Chain. It would be valuable, at this point, for you to consider your own story and to create your own Supply Chain model that focuses on the elements and processes that are critical to your organization.

Supply Chain Management Integration*

SCM focuses on the time efficient movement of resources and the integration of the various functions and pressures that play on those resources. In this section, we will focus on that integration.

The development of an Integrated Supply Chain Strategy is a component of the overall international production, operations, logistics, and distribution strategy. This section will address the international factors that affect successful SCM. It focuses on the integration of the supplier, the logistics

---

* Pieces of this material were taken from the author's book: Plenert, Gerhard, *International Operations Management*, Copenhagen Business School Press, Copenhagen, Denmark, 2002. Reprinted in India by Ane Books, New Delhi, 2003. This book offers an extensive expansion of these fundamental SCM concepts.

system, manufacturing, and customer service of total SCM. It focuses on the following key issues:

The Strategic Framework
Cycle Time and Response Time as the Key Strategic Issues
The Global Supply Chain
Information Integration
Risk Management
Logistics Management

The strategic structure that provides the foundation for SCM is critical in defining corporate performance, as is witnessed by the increasing number of CEOs that are coming from the ranks of operations. Running a company strictly by the financial numbers has proven to be short sighted. Operational measures of performance are being used more frequently.

Strategically, managing the Supply Chain requires looking at management from a broader perspective. Traditionally we were only concerned with the environment immediately around us. Later, we broadened that perspective. We felt that managing the source would allow us to run a leaner production environment with lower inventory levels. More recently, we have recognized the need to look even more broadly to the management of the entire source supply (the suppliers' supplier) through the entire demand/customer network (the customer's customer). Managers do not take over the responsibility of everyone in the Supply Chain. Rather, they integrate the information network so that all elements of the Supply Chain can uniformly interact and extract information from the same supply network. The Internet has become a tool for the interchange of SCM activity. It moves us away from a traditional point-to-point information exchange to a more connected, interactive information exchange where all elements of the Supply Chain can continuously monitor the performance of the overall supply network.

Traditionally we would take a slightly different approach to the supplier to customer relationship. The line for vendor to customer was more linear and direct. The process was more simplistic and more controlled. It was difficult to manage the logistics and sourcing process in any other way than by having the producer controlling the entire process. However, more

Supply Chain Management Approach

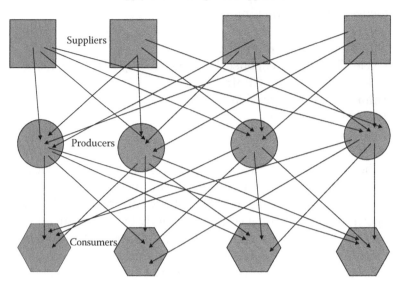

Chart 2.7 Supply Chain Approach

recent Supply Chain environments look more like Chart 2.7 where we see the SCM approach. In this process, we see the sharing of information and a form of integrated interdependence (integrated in that all the components are connected to the information network, independent in that a level of trust must exist between the organizations that allow each of them to manage their own piece of the relationship).

The benefits of this type of integration include:

Greatly reduced inventories because the Supply Chain manages inventory movement
Lower safety stock levels
Greatly reduced cycle times
Increased customer responsiveness
A more participative management approach
Greater information accessibility at all nodes in the Supply Chain
Significant cost reductions
More price and delivery competitiveness, which is extremely important when dealing with products that are at the mature stage of the product lifecycle

Fewer intermediaries and promotional costs in the sales transaction

More direct customer problem responsiveness and problem resolution

Better quantitative indicators for all elements of the Supply Chain

The disadvantages of SCM include:

Loss of direct control of internal information

Loss of information secrecy

Ineffectiveness of the remainder of the Supply Chain to integrate

Loss of management control of the overall process

Because of the elimination of inventory buffers at each step in the Supply Chain, a failure in the Supply Chain is often more catastrophic

In developing a strategy that focuses on SCM, the methodology of information integration becomes critical. Also critical is the connectivity and relationships between sources and customers. This would not work well in a management environment that focuses on control and authoritarianism.

Another strategic element in SCM that needs to be managed is "time." The Supply Chain network reacts quickly to changes. For example, in the Toyota Supply Chain, a customized car can be ordered in the morning and come rolling off the production line later that same day. This type of "integrated SCM network" responsiveness requires the integrated management of not just the facility but also of all suppliers.

From this discussion, we have seen that a Supply Chain approach to international industrial management affects all the competitive strategic priorities. These are:

Cost—Reduced because of reduced inventory levels and lower sales costs.

Service—Increased because of shorter cycle times, which increase customer responsiveness.

Flexibility—Shorter cycle times offer more flexibility in product customization and product mix performance.

Quality—The Supply Chain approach is closer to the JIT flow because of reduced cycle times, which means that product defects or errors are caught faster, which allows corrective action to be quicker. More importantly, the Supply Chain approach integrates not just time, quantity, and delivery information, but also integrates quality specifications and standards so that everyone is on the same page as far as customer expectations are concerned.

Cycle Time and Response Time as the Key Strategic Metric

Time is critically important in a global strategic Supply Chain network. It is the key to competitive success. SCM together with segmentation methodologies reduces cycle time and therefore improves response time to customer concerns and expectations. Because of these reasons, an organization that is not part of an integrated Supply Chain cannot be an effective competitor in the next decade.

The Global Supply Chain

Thus far, we have focused on the operational workings of the three resources in a Supply Chain. We will next focus on some of the various forces that affect the performance of the Supply Chain. Some of these forces include:

Political forces—Government restrictions and expectations with which you will need to work.

Technology forces—Technological changes in both product technology (which product is competitive and where the product is on the product lifecycle) and process technologies (the best shipping methods, warehousing methods, or manufacturing methods). The costs of these technologies and their level of development vary all over the world. Some costs are regionally dependent like labor prices, levels of education, or capital equipment costs and others are not regional. For example, if we are shipping by container, the shipping cost from Los Angeles to San Francisco is nearly the same as the cost of shipping from Singapore to San Francisco because the majority of the cost comes in handling the containers, not in moving them.

Market forces—Market interests and demands can vary significantly from region to region. For example, the demand for crosses in Saudi Arabia is zero because of legal restrictions in the country, but in Italy, the demand could be very strong. Demand will also vary significantly as countries migrate from under-developed, to developing, and then to developed status.

With all of these considerations, we can easily come up with a long list of some of the increased complexities of integrating into a global Supply Chain network. Some of these include:

Geography—Distance tends to slow down the Supply Chain. For example, trucking products in China is quite different from trucking them in the United States. Additionally, some areas have infrastructures that are difficult to access, like poor roads, poor power, or poor telephone landlines.

Information—Not all areas of the world have infrastructures that are effective enough to facilitate Internet access.

Training levels including language skills—Not all areas have the same standards and expectations from their employees. For example, the education levels in India, in some regions, are higher than in the United States. Additionally, specifications and documentation can be misinterpreted if language skills are lacking. For example, the United States' insistence on using inches has more than once caused products to be produced in meters. Even NASA has encountered unit of measure discrepancies in some of their flights.

Demand forecasting becomes more challenging—Demand trends cannot be patterned after the United States in different cultures and environments. Moreover, often there is no local demand history upon which to base forecast estimates.

Economic factors—Exchange rate variations can significantly affect the profitability of a transaction. A minor variation in the exchange rate can destroy the profit margins. Therefore, it becomes important to standardize the Supply Chain on a common, stable currency. However, the negative effect of this standardization is that the local manufacturer may be driven out of business because the exchange rate variations can drive his operating costs up substantially. There is a level of economic risk associated with the international Supply Chain transaction that did not previously exist in a strictly domestic supply chain.

Technology—Levels vary significantly from region to region and from country to country.

Quality—The expectations on quality can vary significantly. Germany defines quality as engineering durability, while Japan defines it as features and functions, and the United States wants economy.

Financial resources—The financial capability to gear up for increased production demand can affect the performance of a supplier.

It is important to note that many of these also become key areas of interest when we discuss various segmentation structures.

Information Integration

As mentioned earlier in this chapter, EDI (Electronic Data Interchange), as a traditional SCM information integration tool, has been replaced by the Internet. By using the Internet, individuals can now do much of their demand shopping through a computer terminal. For example, if you need a book, you go to the Internet and type "Amazon.com" and you have immediate access to a bookstore that is more complete than anything available to you by direct shopping. Moreover, the prices are competitive because they avoid the overhead that a brick-and-mortar bookstore requires. Additionally, they can direct ship the book of your choice to you in only a few days. This does not replace the need for someone to occasionally go to a Barnes and Noble outlet in search of a new book on a subject of interest. Sometimes it is fun just to go shopping. However, the Internet saves a tremendous amount of time in the area of demand shopping.

As a consumer, you can purchase products from all over the world through the Internet. You have the ability to access suppliers that had previously been completely out of your reach. You can evaluate and compare products in ways that had previously been impossible. And you can do it without the cost of travel, sales, and marketing.

The retailing benefits are just a small part of the potential benefits of the Internet. In the area of SCM, we have already discussed how the Internet allows integrated information access between suppliers, manufacturers, distributors, retailers, and even the end consumer. This information integration opens up a new world of information sharing between these links of the Supply Chain, which should also build confidence between the various elements.

The Internet does not eliminate the need for internal, intranet systems. Internal production processes still need to be managed using the traditional MRP, JIT, DRP, etc., management tools. These need to be evaluated carefully to satisfy the requirements of the local operation. The input and outputs of these internal systems require access to the Internet for information exchange. For example, a customer's placement of an order would trigger all of the following:

1. Open a purchase requisition at the customer's site.
2. Open a sales order at the retailer's location.
3. Open a purchase requisition at the retailer for a purchase from the manufacturer.
4. Open a sales order at the manufacturer for the retailer's product.

5. Open a shipment requisition with the shipper for the scheduled due date.
6. Open a purchase requisition at the manufacturer for the materials needed to build the product—this could be several requisitions for several sets of materials.
7. Open a work order for the production process to begin when all the materials become available.
8. Open a sales order with each of the respective vendors.
9. Open a shipment requisition for each of the materials to be shipped to the manufacturer.
10. Open a materials requisition at each supplier location for the materials needed at each location.

From this example, it is easy to see the interconnectivity that occurs with the placement of an order. All of this information is then needed to drive the internal information mechanisms.

Risk Management

In the global Supply Chain transaction, there is the need for a great deal of trust. There is trust in the reliability of the information, trust in the logistics mechanisms, trust in the political stability, trust in the financial mechanisms, like the exchange rate fluctuations, etc. This trust is built up over time. It is not automatic. Internationally we often find that relationships are more important than contractual agreements. In some countries, the spoken agreement is more legally binding then the signed document. Failure in any of these trusts creates transactional risk, and this risk needs to be assessed. An entire gradient of risk levels in which organizations are willing to engage ranges from risk averse to risk taking. Generally, the reason for taking on an increased level of risk is for the increased potential of gain that comes with the risk. In this section, I will discuss several areas of risk and how these risks can be segmented in order to improve how well they are managed. However, this discussion is not intended to be a comprehensive discussion of all the elements of risk assessment. That would be a book all by itself.

Political risk is assessed and measured in several international data banks. For example, the CIA evaluates the political stability of a country and assigns a risk value to this assessment. Similarly, the international monetary organizations like the World Bank and the IMF (International Monetary Fund) evaluate and assess the financial risk of all the countries in the world. These risk assessment values are extremely valuable in international transactions. However, these are easier risks to assess because we have individuals and organizations developing these assessments for us. It is more difficult to assess the risks associated with markets, and their reactions to issues like foreign products and international trends. For example, a defined trend shows how markets in the United States follow the trends in London, and Japan follows the trends in the United States.

Reactions to your product are often extremely difficult to predict. For example, competitive reactions, government reactions, vendor reactions, or customer reactions have been known to dramatically affect product acceptance. We hear of stories like the difficulty of selling a very successful American car, the Nova, in Mexico because in Spanish the name means "no go." Or the reverse, when a Mexican producer tried to sell a very popular Mexican sandal in the United States people were offended by the name "Jesus shoe."

The objective of managing risk is to minimize the exposure to unforeseen and unplanned-for risks destroying profitability. If you are a risk-adverse organization, then you need to minimize all the excessive risk factors. If you are a risk-taking organization, then you want to identify and account for as much of the risk as possible so that your financial returns are sufficient to justify the risk taken. The importance of risk and risk assessment strongly affects operational performance and should be carefully considered.

When considering segmentation, we may consider risk segments. There may be products or market areas that contain higher levels of risk causing us to vary our approach to that market. We may use different planning or marketing mechanisms based on our anticipated level of risk.

Logistics Management

Logistics management, which includes the transport of goods and the warehousing of them, is an extremely large piece of the SCM puzzle. Without the efficient flow of the logistics process, all the gains of manufacturing efficiency are erased. For example, Toyota can manufacture a car in four hours. Then it takes weeks and sometimes months to move the product to the overseas retailer. That is why the flow of this logistics process has become so critical that the Supply Chain can be ineffective without properly managing it.

Summary

A Supply Chain is movement, specifically, the movement of three key resources: materials, information, and money. The movement of these resources is affected by a series of forces that interact with the overall Supply Chain. The objective is to make the entire Supply Chain as seamless as possible to the customer, while at the same time integrating all the operational complexities of the Supply Chain into an optimized, well-performing machine.

> We are today less technology driven and more driven to solve business problems. In order to solve business problems, you need to understand the business very well. You may apply technology, and you may not. It may be a process change, it may be a people initiative, and where technology is required, you need to be able to bring it to the plate.
>
> **David Johns, Senior Vice President/CIO,**
> **and Chief Supply Chain Officer, Owens Corning**[*]

---

[*] Barney, Doug. Owens Corning builds for the future, *CSCO*, August, 2005, pp. 10–15.

References

Burt, David, Donald Dobler, and Steven Starling. *World Class Supply Management*ˢᵐ, 7th ed., Boston, MA: McGraw-Hill Irwin, 2003.

Plenert, Gerhard. *International Operations Management*, Copenhagen, Denmark: Copenhagen Business School Press, 2002. Reprinted in India by Ane Books, New Delhi, 2003.

Plenert, Gerhard. *Plant Operations Deskbook*, Homewood, IL: Business 1 IRWIN, 1993.

Plenert, Gerhard. *The SCM Manager: Value Chain Management in an eCommerce World*, Los Angeles, CA: Blackhall Publishing, 2001.

Semler, Ricardo. *Maverick: The Success Story Behind the World's Most Unusual Workplace*, New York: Warner Books, 1993.

3
Performance Measures[*]

We must use time wisely and forever realize that the time is always ripe to do right.

Nelson Mandela

In a conversation about Performance Metrics we always need to start by asking the question, "What is our goal?" Are we looking to be the best in customer service? Are we looking to control market share? Are we worried about costs, like inventory costs or operating costs? Or are we focused on quality? Each of these goals drives us toward different methodologies and they can create conflicting priorities.

Once we have defined our goals, we can start our search for metrics. The metric we select needs to be one that not only measures but also more importantly motivates us toward our goal.

If it can't be measured, then it won't be improved!

The Role and Purpose of Measures

Recently, I attended a meeting with a General in the Hawaii National Guard and his comment was, "We have been making

---

[*] Some sections of this chapter were taken from the books *Reinventing Lean: Introducing Lean Management Into the Supply Chain*, Elsevier Science, 2007, and *International Operations Management*, Copenhagen Business School Press, Copenhagen, Denmark, 2002. Reprinted in India by Ane Books, New Delhi, 2003. Included by permission from the author Gerhard Plenert.

changes and improvements for years. But I have no idea if anything is running any better. People keep telling me its better, but I really don't know if it's better or not. I have no measures that would convince me that anything is better." It is an excellent and insightful question. How do we know something has improved if there isn't a measurable way of showing how or what has improved? If you say something has improved, then how do you demonstrate the improvement through quantifiable results? This requires some form of metric or it is simply meaningless hearsay.

As mentioned in the last chapter, measures are critical to a successfully performing Supply Chain enough so for a discussion of metrics to warrant its own chapter. Measures are not a tool for data collection. They are not implemented because accounting wants another piece of information. They are only implemented when they add value to the process.

For example, Signetics Corporation manufactures electronics components. A reduction in sales forced them to identify one of their plants for closure so they selected the plant with the lowest quality performance, which happened to be in Provo, Utah. After the plant had been slated for closure, some of its managers asked me to come in and review (post-mortem) why their quality was so poor. They wanted to learn from their mistakes so that they would not repeat them in the future (at their new job).

After some lengthy discussions, it was easy for an outsider like me to identify the cause of the failure. They had implemented Six Sigma, TQM, and a variety of other quality initiatives. They had banners on the walls and extensive training programs. They had meetings and activities around these quality initiatives. However, their quality was still the poorest of all the plants, and they could not understand why, until I asked them questions about their measurement system. I asked them what their performance measurements were for employee performance. They answered that it was "piece parts produced." These employees received a performance bonus based on the number of units produced, not on whether the parts were any good. Quality was the responsibility of the quality department and was often corrected and fixed after the fact. Moreover, the line employees madly pumped out parts. Therefore, no matter how well publicized and trained the line workers were on quality, the bottom line is that it did not help the paycheck and therefore the employees were not that interested in all the "quality stuff."

Philosophically speaking, the only valid reason for a measurement system is motivation. No matter what you measure, the simple fact that you are measuring it draws attention to it. It will encourage employees to think that it is important to management and therefore they will do their best to make those numbers look good. And employees can be very good at making numbers look good. So, if it is not important, or, as in the Signetics case, if the measurement detracts from the results you really want, then it is a bad measure. We need to eliminate that measure and only implement measures that truly add value.

Some Examples of Supply Chain Improvements

Having established the importance and role of measures, we should now recognize the direct relationship between metrics and Supply Chain performance. Looking at Chart 3.1, we see examples of the types of process improvements that are typically

Supply Chain Improvements

Typical Quantified Benefits from Integrating the Supply Chain	
➤Delivery Performance	✓15%–30% Improvement
➤Inventory Reduction	✓25%–70% Improvement
➤Fulfillment Cycle Time	✓30%–50% Reduction
➤Forecast Accuracy	✓20%–80% Improvement
➤Overall Productivity	✓10%–20% Improvement
➤Lower Supply-Chain Costs	✓25%–50% Improvement
➤Fill Rates	✓20%–30% Improvement
➤Improved Capacity	✓10%–40% Increase

Chart 3.1 Supply Chain Benefits

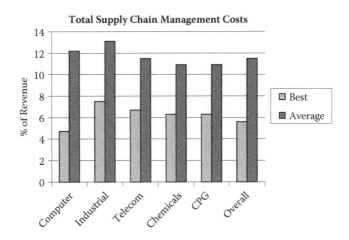

Chart 3.2 Supply Chain Costs

experienced by Supply Chain improvements. These numbers are repeated again and again in journals, magazines, and conference presentations. In fact, most of these numbers are conservative and the author has successfully beaten many of these numbers.

Digging a little deeper into our example, we would consider Supply Chain Costs. Looking at Chart 3.2, we see industry averages for the cost of the Supply Chain. For example, looking at the computer industry, we see that the difference between the industry average and the best of class is more than 7 percent of revenue. This goes directly to the bottom line. What company wouldn't want an additional 7 percent net profit boost (which is more than many companies earn in total)?

Looking at another important measure of Supply Chain performance—cycle time—we realize that there are several different types of cycle time. The most obvious one, the one that most organizations benchmark against, is the amount of time it takes to produce a product from start to finish. Supply Chain examples of cycle time include the amount of time it takes from the start of the Supply Chain through to the delivery of the finished product to the end customer.

Any measure of cycle time/processing time is valuable as an indicator of Supply Chain performance. One specific and critically important example that often is not even considered is cash-to-cash cycle time (see Chart 3.3). Cash-to-cash cycle time

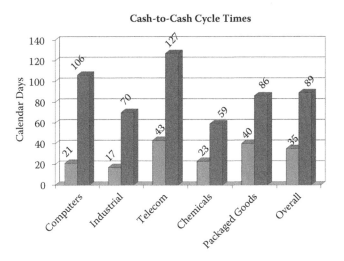

Cash-to-Cash Cycle Times

Chart 3.3 Cash-to-Cash Cycle Times

is the amount of time it takes from the time you pay for the
materials until the time you receive the cash payment from the
customer. It is the amount of time your cash flow is tied up. It is
the amount of time you have to finance the cost of having that
cash tied up. And this can be quite an expensive investment
for a company. Let us again take a look at the computer industry in Chart 3.3 as an example of what this means. Industry
average cash-to-cash cycle time is 106 days. In an industry as
volatile and dynamic as the computer industry, this could be
suicide. Computer equipment can become obsolete very rapidly. When compared to the "best of class" average, we see it
down to 21 days. The difference is 85 days. If we consider a
$1,000 computer, with an inventory holding cost of 7 percent,
this would be an increase in cost per computer of $16.30.
However, just for the sake of analysis, we can go even further
and look at the best of the "best of class," Dell Computers. Here
we find an interesting situation. Dell has a cash-to-cash cycle
time of minus seven days. Dell receives payment from the customer over the Internet prior to the time when it purchases
the materials from the vendor. Dell's cash flow days advantage
is 113 days when compared to the industry average, which
equates to $21.67 financing cost advantage per $1,000 unit.
Dell receives the additional benefit of running its operation

using its customers' cash flow. Additionally, it does not have to build up any inventory of finished goods that are just standing on hold waiting for orders to be placed the way other computer vendors do. This equates to a significant cost and cash flow advantage against most of Dell's competitors in the industry.

Another outstanding example of an organization that effectively optimizes cash flow is Walmart. It has managed and optimized its Supply Chain logistics to the point that it often sells the product at the retail outlet before it purchased the product from its vendor. For example, if the payment cycle for a product is net 30 days after delivery, but it can get the product to the store and get it sold in anything less than 30 days, it results in a positive cash flow.

Dell and Walmart are excellent examples of how segmentation of products and customers can be managed to the point where it has a significant and direct impact on the organization's profitability.

The Role and Purpose of Control Systems

Control systems seem to become an organizational obsession. For example, in the pharmaceutical industry, where pills are being produced, there is the tendency to fix problems and failures by adding controls. In one particular organization, the cleaning and purification of equipment had experienced several failures and the solution was to add several additional quality checks. They would have the equipment cleaned. Then they would have a co-worker inspect the cleaning. Then they would have a manager inspect the inspection. Then they would have quality repeat the inspection process again. The failure in this repetitive process was that the only person who was certified in inspecting the cleaning process was the person originally doing the cleaning. Because there was no documentation on what defined a clean machine, everyone else was just checking what he or she thought was important. The extra checks were irrelevant and non-value added.

Another example that I recently encountered on a different project was with an oil and gas giant. In this case, they required 16 signatures to approve each individual purchase order. Each signature was a validation checkpoint on the approval process. When we asked someone in the middle or near the end of the list, "What criteria do you use to decide if you should approve this purchase order?" the response was, "I trust these other people that are signing and if they think this is a good idea then I go along with it." But if we asked one of the first couple of people on the list the same question, their response was, "These other individuals on the list are more qualified to evaluate this purchase order so I sign it in order to get it passed on to the people that really know what they're looking at." As a result, no one even looked at the details behind the purchase order. The excessive number of controls caused less control rather than more control, and the existence of the controls themselves was generating extensive delays and a failure in the validation process.

Another interesting example was a manufacturer of high-tech parts that had numerous measurement systems to measure quality performance. They incorporated control systems like Statistical Process Control (SPC), which, in and of itself, is a very good system when applied as a performance enhancement tool used to measure process performance "as it happens." But as a control system, which was "after the fact," it had no effect on quality output. All it did was confirm that indeed a defect had occurred. It identified a varying number of areas where errors occurred, but it did little to aid in identifying solutions.

We are left with the following slogan:

Inappropriately applied control systems are the enemy of an efficient supply chain environment.

Experience has taught us that the implementation of control systems results in:

- Adding steps to the process
- Increasing the opportunities for failure because there are now more steps in the process
- Increasing the overall cycle time
- Misdirecting employees on what is important in achieving overall goals

- Wasted resources (time, floor space, etc.)
- Wasted capacity
- Most importantly, they move the error to somewhere else in the process rather than fix or eliminate the error

In an example of a different project that involved a government parts validation lab, one of the first activities we conducted with the lab was to flowchart the entire First Article process. In doing so, the team members were able to identify a large number of intersections in the communications flow. About one-third of these were the results of failures in the process. In fact, its main customer, the DLA (Defense Logistics Agency) had initiated a data collection and control process that increased the First Article processing time by 4 to 10 hours per part. All of these extra steps were the results of information flow failures and they resulted in control systems that had a significant impact on the overall process flow time, which had reached an average of 141 days per part. By focusing on improving the communications network, they were able to eliminate many of the unnecessary communications and checkpoints, and after just six months were able to reduce flow time down to 85 days. Other activities followed, which reduced the flow time even more. It is interesting to see the large impact that improving communications and eliminating unnecessary control and checkpoints were able to have on the number of controls and how they were able to generate a significant impact on flow/cycle time.

What Is the Best Measure for Your Organization?

Numerous effective measures of Supply Chain performance exist, the best being focused on:

1. Cycle time, which offers inventory reductions and capacity increases

2. On-time performance to customer expectations (like on-time delivery to the customer's initially requested delivery date)
3. Quality, which is the foundational building block of a satisfied customer base

Other metric options can be seen in Chart 3.1. However, the most important criterion for an effective measurement system in any Supply Chain environment is that it is focused on motivating the correct response from the employee base. When we consider segmentation process and principles in the next chapters, we will find more measures that are valuable in optimizing a Supply Chain. However, the measure that will fit your organization the best depends on the following:

The goals of the organization
The expectations of the customer
The response that employees or suppliers will have to the measure
The accessibility and reliability of the measure

You start by looking at these criteria for a measurement system and then you attempt to identify as few measures as possible that will drive everyone's response toward optimizing that measure. You should never base your measurement system on tradition. An appropriate and effective measure may be challenging to identify, but it will be surprising how directly it can affect overall organization performance.

Summary

In an attempt to use Information Technology (IT) to enable the global SCM of a micro-motor manufacturing company headquartered in Hong Kong, the KE Group was commended by financial analysts as one of the few local companies that was unaffected by the Asian economic crisis. The reported, measurable results of this implementation included a 43.3 percent growth in net profit with only an 8 percent increase in sales.[*]

The KE Group example and the many other examples presented in this chapter have demonstrated the type of improvements that can be achieved by implementing a Segmented Supply Chain, which correctly applies strategically focused goals and metrics and minimizes the use of "waste" control points.

Without meaningful measures, you will achieve your goal: *no meaningful results*. And with incorrect measures, you will receive incorrect results. The selection and proper implementation of a measurement system is critical to successful use of segmentation in SCM.

References

Plenert, Gerhard. *International Operations Management*, Copenhagen Business School Press, Copenhagen, Denmark, 2002. Reprinted in India by Ane Books, New Delhi, 2003.

Plenert, Gerhard. *The eManager: Value Chain Management in an eCommerce World*, Los Angeles, CA: Blackhall Publishing, 2001.

---

[*] Taken from a 2005 IRMA presentation in San Diego titled "IT Enabled Global Supply Chain Management: A Case Study" by Narasimhaiah Gorla, Administrative Staff College of India, Harish Verma, Wayne State University, and Tam Wai Chou, Hong Kong Polytechnic Institute, Hong Kong.

4

Analytics and SCS

Competition is the keen cutting edge of business, always shaving away at costs.

Henry Ford

What was true in Henry Ford's day is exponentially true today. The level of competition has risen from local to global, placing enormous stress on both the private and the public sectors alike. The ability to accurately identify barriers to success, define the strategies to overcome those barriers, and then focus the limited resources that every organization has on executing those strategies is what differentiates the organization that controls its future from the one that fails.

The urgency for effective business analytics has never been more evident as can be seen by the emphasis that organizations like Aberdeen's research place on studying analytics. Aberdeen shows a growing number of business leaders driving analytical projects and putting their stamp on the decision-making culture of the organization. By managing the correct mix of capabilities for managing and exploiting Big Data (the buzzword for big volumes of detailed and generally unmanaged data) and by leveraging visually solutions like BI (Business Intelligence), top companies are boosting performance and optimizing competitiveness.

Math and statistics have traditionally been avoided in making business decisions. Recently organizations have found these tools to be competitive game changers and have incorporated these tools, now renamed analytics, in all aspects of their business from forecasting to customer service level enhancement, to inventory optimization.

When segmentation is introduced, especially in the complex supply chain world that this book is discussing, SCS optimization is impossible without an analytics backbone. As the readers go through this book, they will see analytics repeatedly playing a role in the planning and scheduling processes, in inventory safety stock and batch size calculations, and in various forecasting calculations.

But before we go any further in highlighting the wonders of analytics, let us first try to define what analytics, sometimes referred to as BI, is and how it works.

Analytics Defined

From Wikipedia, the free encyclopedia, we get a definition that analytics is the discovery and communication of meaningful patterns in data. It is especially valuable in areas rich with recorded information, which requires extensive computation, referred to as Big Data. Analytics relies on the simultaneous application of statistics, computer programming and analysis tools, and the mathematics of operations research to quantify and evaluate performance. However, analytics is not just number crunching. It also includes the presentability of the information. Executives want graphics, dashboards, scorecards, and data visualization to be used to communicate any insights that are achieved.

Firms apply analytics to business data to describe, predict, and improve business performance. Traditional retail areas, which are the focus of analytics, include organizational transformation, enterprise decision management, retail analytics, store assortment and SKU optimization, marketing optimization and marketing mix analytics, web analytics, sales force sizing and optimization, price and promotion modeling, predictive science, risk analysis, and fraud analytics. Analytics often requires extensive Big Data computation and applies algorithms and software to optimize the most current methods in computer science, statistics, and mathematics.

Analytics uses descriptive and predictive models to gain valuable knowledge from data while at the same time it uses this insight to recommend action or to guide business decision making. Analytics is not just a tool focused on individual analyses or analysis steps. Analytics is about the overall methodology with a focus on business decisions as the ultimate goal, which defines success.

Level of Analytics and Business Intelligence (BI)

In the book *Competing on Analytics* by Davenport and Harris, we find a graphic that compares an organization's competitive advantage with its degree of BI. It lists the levels of BI as (from lowest to highest):

- Standard reporting
- Ad hoc reporting
- Queries with drill downs
- Alerts
- Statistical analysis
- Forecasting/extrapolation
- Predictive modeling
- Optimization

Using these categories, the first four are considered to be normal access and reporting capabilities, but the last four are considered to be analytics capabilities. The first three talk about past events, specifically Who, What, When, Where, and How. The fourth item (Alerts) focuses on "What is happening now?" The last four talk about root causes and future decisions, specifically Why and What is Next. This analysis clearly defines the difference between simply reporting the facts, and being able to make analytically informed decisions.

How Analytics Is Used

Since retailing is the founder of analytics and is still the primary user of this tool, it is valuable to see how the retail business sector has applied the tool to its day-to-day operations. A few examples of analytics applications include:

Marketing optimization—Marketing has become highly data-driven. Marketing organizations use analytics to determine the success of marketing campaigns. They analyze their success at guiding customer decision making and then use this information to guide internal corporate decisions for investment and consumer targeting. Marketing analytics tools include demographic studies, customer segmentation, etc., thereby allowing marketers to make better decisions and to successfully communicate those decisions.

Web analytics—Web analytics allows marketers to collect detailed information about website transactions. Those website interactions provide the web analytics information systems with the information critically needed to track their preferences, buying tendencies, etc. It uses keywords, IP address, and website visitor activities. This information is critical and allows the marketers to improve their marketing campaigns.

Modeling—Analysis techniques use models to evaluate marketing mix, pricing and promotion, sales force optimization, customer analysis, and segmentation. A focus on digital media has slightly changed the vocabulary so that marketing mix modeling is commonly referred to as attribution modeling. These tools and techniques support strategic marketing decisions such as overall spend and how to allocate budgets. More tactical analytics support offers information in terms of targeting the best potential customer with the optimal message in the most cost effective medium at the ideal time.

Portfolio analysis—Another application of business analytics looks at the portfolio. A bank or lending agency may have a collection of accounts of varying value and risk. The accounts may differ by various segment categories. The lender balances the return on the loan with the potential risk of default. Analytics answers these questions and looks at how to evaluate the portfolio as a whole.

Risk analytics—Predictive models have been widely developed to bring certainty across the risk scores for individual customers. Credit scores have been built to predict borrowers' delinquency behavior. Scores are also widely used to evaluate the credit worthiness of applicants.

Big Data—In commercial analytics, the emphasis is on solving the challenges of analyzing massive, complex data sets. Often such data is in a constant state of change. These sets of data are referred to as Big Data. Today Big Data is a problem for many businesses that operate transactional systems online and amass large volumes of data quickly.

Unstructured Data—Another area of analytics focuses on unstructured data. This is data where the format varies widely and cannot be stored in traditional relational databases without exerting a significant effort on data transformation. Sources of unstructured data, such as email, the contents of word processor documents, etc., are rapidly becoming a relevant source of BI for businesses, governments, and universities.

Moving beyond retailing, analytics is increasingly being used in education. The complexity of student performance analytics presents challenges. Educators try to understand and use analytics to discern patterns in student performance to predict graduation likelihood, improve chances of student success, etc. An entire test publication industry has been built around test validation and test score normalization.

Analytics Strategy

A recent article by Dan Besset, Program Vice President of Business Analytics, published in *IDC Analyst Connection* (www.idc.com) describes the need for a strategy for any analytics processes. He suggests that a growing number of organizations are moving toward analytics or BI systems by turning to evidence-based decision-making supported by a range of BI and analytics technology and processes. These tools enable decision makers to have the best possible intelligence about customers, finances, operations, suppliers, and the market.

IDC claims that a higher BI and analytics competency and pervasiveness will be achieved when organizational culture, business processes, and technologies are designed and implemented with the goal of improving or automating all strategic, operational, and tactical decision-making capabilities for all stakeholders. However, BI and analytics technology and projects cannot be ends in themselves. They exist to provide support to decision makers or to automate certain decision-making processes. These must lead to actions.

IDC encourages organizations to develop an organization-wide BI and analytics strategy that articulates responses to questions like (for the full set of questions go to the article on the IDC website):

- What are our organization's business objectives, challenges, and goals, and how do we measure progress toward these goals?
- Are your BI objectives aligned with your business objectives? What metrics or key performance indicators (KPIs) exist to ensure that measurement of progress toward organizational goals is made possible?
- What are the types of strategic, operational, and tactical decisions being made at different levels in your organization?
- What technology components exist or are needed to ensure that the decision support or automation needs of all decision makers are addressed?

Responses to these questions will assist in defining a long-term BI and analytics strategy.

IDC claims that its studies have shown that indicators that define BI and analytics competency and pervasiveness have a direct correlation to the competitiveness of organizations within their respective industries. Other IDC studies have identified the median ROI of BI and analytics projects to be just over 100 percent, while the benefits accrued by organizations deploying BI and analytics technology and processes are split up as follows:

54 percent from business process improvements
42 percent from productivity gains
4 percent from technology cost savings

Therefore, 96 percent of the benefits are in the productivity and business process enhancement categories. IDC research demonstrates that organizations focused on BI and analytics are more competitive than nonusers are. Eighty percent of the most competitive organizations are users.

Analytics and BI Applications

The application domains for analytics in business can best be mapped out using a Lean/Six Sigma tool called the SIPOC (Supplier-Input-Process-Output-Customer) map. In Chart 4.1, we see a SIPOC map for the potential uses of analytics.

As we can see from this map, analytics in a Supply Chain covers a lot more than just marketing. It can affect all areas of the business. It directly influences decision-making throughout most of the business processes.

Analytics and Supply Chain Segmentation (SCS)

In their book *Analytics at Work* (p. 81) Davenport, Harris, and Morison created a model for the application of Supply Chain analytics, which highlights the analytical questions and the appropriate Supply Chain tool that would offer a solution. This

SIPOC for Analytics

Supplier	Input	Process	Output	Customer
• Supplier performance analysis • Supplier location analysis • Supplier risk analysis • Competitive analysis • Supplier segmentation	• On time delivery performance • Quality performance • Inventory optimization/Kanban/consigned stock/VMIs • Supply side segmentation	• Financial analysis/NPV • Manufacturing planning and scheduling • Inventory optimization • R&D value generation • HR utilization/staffing optimization • Product segmentation	• Product mix planning • Logistics/routing optimization • Distribution management • Demand side segmentation	• Customer demographics • Customer segmentation • Marketing assessments

Chart 4.1 SIPOC

Analytics Supply Chain Examples

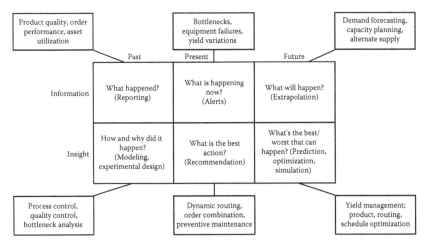

Chart 4.2 Supply Chain Analytics

model can be seen in Chart 4.2 (a detailed explanation of the model can be found in their book).

This model gives us the analytics analysts' perspective of the types of tools that can be applied in a Supply Chain environment. Another way to look at this is to consider the perspective

The Symptoms of a Suboptimal Supply Chain

Supply Chain

Procurement
- Suboptimal contract pricing for materials
- More spot buying

Manufacturing
- Strain on manufacturing agility
- Excessive overtime and higher turnover
- Increased maintenance costs

Distribution/Logistics
- Higher freight costs
- Less favorable contract terms
- Higher carrying costs
- Lower inventory turns
- Poor working cap utilization
- High SLOB (separate line of business) levels

Demand Chain

Marketing
- Promotion cannibalization
- Suboptimal NPL
- Decreased mindshare & shelf space

Sales
- Chasing shipments not orders
- Allocations & lost sales
- Higher discounts for SLOB (separate line of business) products
- Less effective volume incentives

Customer
- Low customer service levels
- Low customer satisfaction
- Service level penalties

Chart 4.3 Suboptimal Supply Chain

of the Supply Chain user. When we look at the overall Supply Chain, we can consider all the areas where Supply Chain decisions occur, and there are a lot. Then we can consider what analytical tools may be available to facilitate the decision-making process and provide solutions to these specific problems. If we look at the various failure points of a Supply Chain we see the issues indicated in Chart 4.3. The impact of suboptimal Supply Chain Management (SCM) is felt across the entire Value Chain. The financial impact of these failures includes:

- Inaccurate revenue and profitability guidance
- Difficulty in evaluating Capital Expenditures and Mergers and Acquisitions (M&As)

From this list of opportunities in Chart 4.3, we can identify myriad areas where analytics can support improved decision-making.

Diving deeper to see even more specific SCM requirements and shortcomings, we can look at an AMR research study that emphasizes the performance areas that are critical to SCM performance. These areas are the ones that have the largest

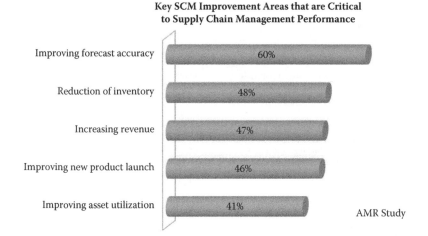

Chart 4.4 SCM Improvement Areas

impact and that currently show the highest level of deficiency. In Chart 4.4, we see that the most critical area is Forecast Accuracy, which can be supported by a large number of analytics tools. The next is Inventory Reduction or Inventory Optimization, which again finds that analytics has a large number of tools and options to facilitate. These first two items will be the subject of a detailed case example that is the subject of the next few chapters.

The consulting world has numerous models of what the optimal Supply Chain should look like. One of these models is called the "Perfect Factory," which is diagrammed in Chart 4.5. In this model, we see various levels of organizational optimization that can be supported by effective analytics. At the highest level, we see the Global View. At this level, we stress Supply Chain Visibility. We need to align the organizational objectives of innovation, performance, and process excellence with the various organizational components of the Supply Chain.

The next level is the Regional View. At this level, we focus on Supply Chain responsiveness in various market segments. This includes product category, organizational cluster, or country structure segmentation. These segments are based on the performance of the Supply Chain to enable and execute around a customer-led Supply Chain model. This model will focus on Supply Chain flexibility and agility in the Supply Chain operations.

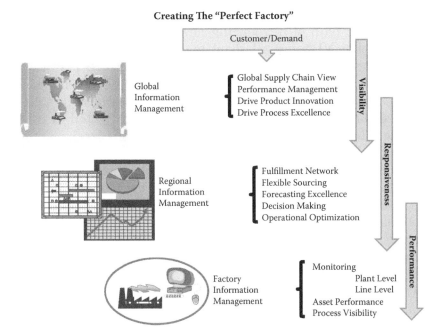

Chart 4.5 Perfect Factory

At the lowest level, this model takes the Plant View. At this level, the focus shifts to real time performance of planned versus actual production. This level is focused on plant execution and KPIs.

Once again, the message is that the Supply Chain is filled with opportunities where analytics can have an enormous impact. At each of these organizational levels, we can see in Chart 4.5 where graphics demonstrate the types of analytical tools that could be applied. Mathematical modeling can prove insight and guidance throughout the Supply Chain to facilitate and guide the decision-making process.

Applied Analytics Case Example

In a recent article by F.A. Lambay, CPIM, CSCP, CPF, which was posted on www.wipro.com, he described an application of analytics in the management of New Product Introductions (NPI).

He describes his article as an explanation of how analytics reduced the pain of introducing new high-tech products. He stresses that NPIs are all about managing product lifecycles by enhancing sales and improving the operational planning process, which in turn helps companies quickly gain market share ahead of the competition. The next few paragraphs summarize some of the key findings that are highlighted in this article. Please review the full article to get more depth.

In this article, Lambay describes how the high-tech industry has always been witnessing shortened product lifecycles and technology cycles. Traditionally, the decision-makers in the Supply Chain have been unwilling to meet the level of collaboration required in an ideal customer-supplier relationship. It became extremely difficult to forecast NPIs from siloed business stakeholders and also when no previous history existed of similar products. This was additionally complicated by slow moving inventory, which became stranded in the Supply Chain. As old products approached their end of life (EOL), demand eroded.

To successfully optimize the Supply Chain and their inventory levels would require a reassessment of Supply Chain variables such as batch sizes, economic order quantities (EOQs), minimum order quantities (MOQs), lead times, and the like. This would need to be coupled with an enhanced Sales & Operational Planning (S&OP) process in responding to the rapidly adapting needs of the marketplace and the changing tastes and preferences of the customers.

Traditionally S&OP is used as a Supply Chain planning model that has been around for over 50 years. A lot has changed since then. For example, transformations have occurred in the sensing/shaping/responding of demand signals, managing suppliers, exploding customer preferences, and, of course, shortened product and technology lifecycles. With products rapidly becoming outdated, especially in the high-tech manufacturing industry, Supply Chain experts are turning to predictive modeling techniques. Smarter analytics are used to tackle these Supply Chain challenges.

Analytics tools can track processes across the Supply Chain, identify gaps, report alerts, forecast future demand, chart trends and buying patterns, and bring together visibility, predictability, and sustainability for customers, manufacturers, and suppliers. Empowered with internalized data that had thus far been relegated to silos, companies can be better equipped with analytics to translate historical lag data into leading indicators with actionable insights. This allows them to rapidly adapt to the needs of customers, facilitating timely product innovation, drastically cutting costs, and gaining market share much faster ahead of competition by moving fast in closing demand-supply gaps.

Cutting costs in the Supply Chain and the gains from inventory reduction affects the bottom line with each new technological breakthrough. However, it is challenging to forecast new product launches with no prior history or ramp-down of EOL especially when the pipeline is clogged with components that are also in decline. This translates into bigger inventory exposure risks for all Supply Chain partners wanting to align their demand and supply plans.

The reasons for new product launch failures includes not just being late to market but also the absence of innovative Supply Chain planning processes to ensure new products reached customers in a timely manner. Better tools and metrics are needed in order to drive focused accountability and responsibility. It becomes critical that all Supply Chain partners can foresee potential issues and take corrective measures to cancel/reschedule promised product deliveries thereby reducing the risk levels.

Huge expenses affect cash flow outlays and working capital from last-time buys/builds (LTB), excess and obsolescence (E&O), platform migrations, and discontinuation liabilities. They tend to increase Supply Chain costs and reduce revenues if not planned properly during the pre-launch timeline.

Looking at Chart 4.6 we see a graphic representation of how responsive demand planning would execute in an EOL or NPI setting. This methodology integrates Supply Chain tools, analytics tools, and S&OP tools to create an integrated model that is responsive to the changes in demand created by rapid turnover products. It is always a better idea to introduce collaboration with a "single number forecast" or "game plan," which all Supply Chain partners can subscribe to irrespective of their position in the supply chain. Additionally, the

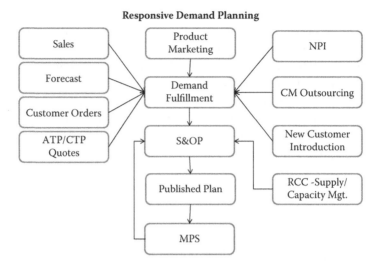

Chart 4.6 Responsive Demand Planning

participation of internal stakeholders and external partners during various stages of new product launches does not end once a new product is launched in the market. Participation must continue throughout the lifecycle.

The enhanced S&OP process in Chart 4.6, which incorporates NPI and EOL, requires analytics and results in greater visibility and predictability. It gives companies the needed insight and confidence to operate with leaner inventory forecasts during the early introductions of new products and the decline of older products.

By integrating NPI and EOL transitioning with analytics and the S&OP process, companies are better equipped to understand and align their risks. These tools identified in Chart 4.7 improve resource allocation, reduce excess inventory, and raise customer service levels. They move away from reactionary demand forecasting toward a proactive responsive tool, which anticipates customer needs from the marketplace and offers unprecedented views into the Supply Chain.

The product lifecycle diagrammed in Chart 4.8 demonstrates the transitioning that occurs as EOL products are phased out and NPI products are introduced. The model described in this article assists in facilitating this transition.

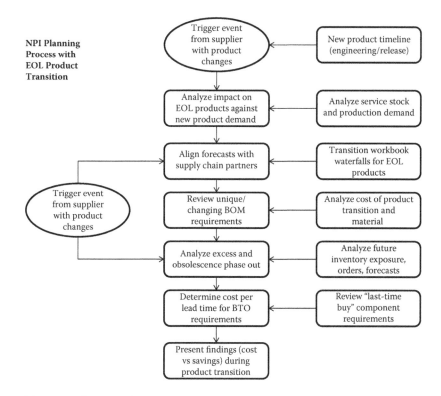

Chart 4.7 NPI Product Planning

Customer Adoption and
Cost Savings tied to PLM
with Enhanced S&OP

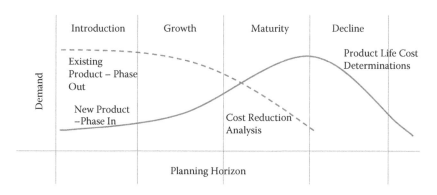

Chart 4.8 Cost Savings Tied to PLM

Some of the business benefits resulting from the new enhanced analytics-based S&OP model were listed in the article as follows:

- Improved delivery schedules
- Increase in market share with speedier time-to-market
- Collaboration throughout entire Supply Chain
- Manufacturing asset efficiency
- Planning cycle time reduction
- Decreased Supply Chain risks
- Lower shipping costs
- Drastic waste reduction
- Improved customer relations
- Maximized revenues

A large percentage of companies that do not have a formal risk managing process would rapidly benefit by implementing the new integrated S&OP process described in this whitepaper. It would allow their businesses to focus on managing exceptions instead of routine fire fighting. I strongly recommend that anyone interested in this topic review the full article as cited earlier.

The article states that integrated business processes that use analytics and apply it to proactive inventory models and forecasts receive value from the essential elements of an enhanced S&OP framework. By using analytics and re-engineering the traditional S&OP process, old products can be easily transitioned into new product introductions limiting inherent Supply Chain risks. The new analytics-inclusive S&OP Process Maturity Model can be used as a diagnostic tool that allows course corrections in financial budgeting, exposing misaligned goals between Supply Chain partners while satisfying customer demand at the lowest total delivered cost.

Summary

This chapter has been a collection of highlights and references defining analytics and demonstrating why its use is critical for successful SCS performance. References have been made to

Aberdeen, Wikipedia, IDC, AMR, and the Davenport/Harris publications, along with several other recently published articles like the Lambay article. Each publication is valuable in its contribution toward an optimal SCS framework.

> Now here, you see, it takes all the running you can do, to keep in the same place. If you want to get somewhere else, you must run at least twice as fast as that.

Lewis Carroll, British mathematician
Through the Looking Glass

References

Davenport, Thomas H., Jeanne G. Harris, and Robert Morison. *Analytics at Work: Smarter Decisions Better Results*, Boston, MA: Harvard Business School Press, 2010.

Davenport, Thomas H., and Jeanne G. Harris. *Competing on Analytics: The New Science of Winning*, Boston, MA: Harvard Business School Press, 2007.

Plenert, Gerhard. *International Operations Management*, Copenhagen Business School Press, Copenhagen, Denmark, 2002. Reprinted in India by Ane Books, New Delhi, 2003.

Simchi-Levi, David. *Operations Rules: Delivering Customer Value through Flexible Operations*, Cambridge, MA: The MIT Press, 2010.

SECTION 2

Segmentation Applied

5

An Applied Example of SCS

The Analysis Process

A pessimist sees the difficulty in every opportunity; an optimist sees the opportunity in every difficulty.

Winston Churchill

Why SCS?*

Segmentation stratifies the end-to-end Supply Chain into logical groups based on the various characteristics of the product, customer, supplier, distribution channel, etc. (see Chart 5.1). These groupings are used to optimize demand and supply planning and scheduling by providing differentiated services for each group. For example, it can be used to group customers with similar fulfillment needs and then develops distinct Supply Chains to meet those needs.

The changing consumer and Supply Chain landscape is driving increasing complexity into product offerings and distribution channels reducing the effectiveness of the Supply Chain. SCS helps to serve each customer and each product at a given point in time while simultaneously maximizing

---

* Portions of this chapter touch on materials that the author personally developed for Wipro Consulting Services and it is being used here by permission.

Product Segmentation

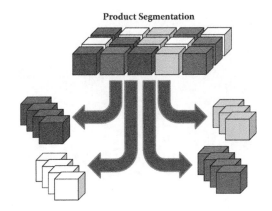

Chart 5.1 Product Segmentation

both customer services and company profitability as it reduces complexity. Chart 5.2 highlights some of the changing dynamics of the Supply Chain where segmentation has affectively impacted performance results.*

Chart 5.3 builds on the identified Supply Chain complexities of Chart 5.2 and describes its impact on a few sample industry segments. It shows specific industry challenges, the drivers that correspond to those challenges, and the various segmentation structures that can be utilized to facilitate reducing or eliminating the pain that corresponds to the listed industry challenges.

Building on the segmentation options listed in Chart 5.3, we take the next step and build out these three listed options, which are:

- Product Segmentation
- Customer Segmentation
- Channel Segmentation

---

* To help the reader with the alphabet soup that is found in this chapter, here is a brief list of some of the terminology that you will encounter, especially in the charts:

BTO—Build to Order
CTO—Configure to Order
FCS—Finite Capacity Scheduling
CTP—Capable to Promise
VMI—Vendor Managed Inventories
ATP—Available to Promise
SCM—Supply Chain Management
CPG—Consumer Packaged Goods
SKU—Stock Keeping Unit
S&OP—Sales and Operations Planning

Why Supply Chain Segmentation (SCS)?

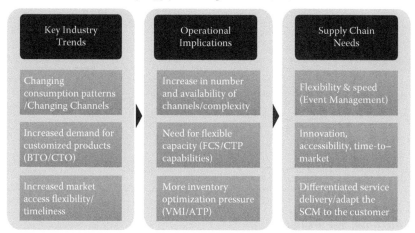

Chart 5.2 Why SCS?

Relevance of SC Segmentation

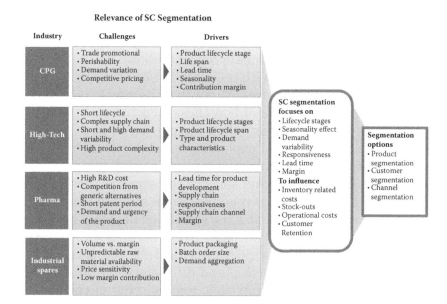

Chart 5.3 Relevance of SCS

Examples of SC Segmentation Types

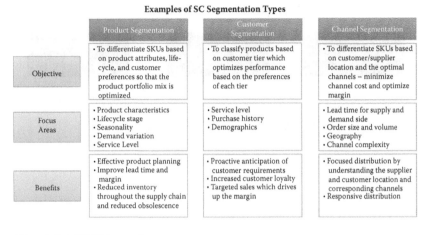

	Product Segmentation	Customer Segmentation	Channel Segmentation
Objective	• To differentiate SKUs based on product attributes, life-cycle, and customer preferences so that the product portfolio mix is optimized	• To classify products based on customer tier which optimizes performance based on the preferences of each tier	• To differentiate SKUs based on customer/supplier location and the optimal channels – minimize channel cost and optimize margin
Focus Areas	• Product characteristics • Lifecycle stage • Seasonality • Demand variation • Service Level	• Service level • Purchase history • Demographics	• Lead time for supply and demand side • Order size and volume • Geography • Channel complexity
Benefits	• Effective product planning • Improve lead time and margin • Reduced inventory throughout the supply chain and reduced obsolescence	• Proactive anticipation of customer requirements • Increased customer loyalty • Targeted sales which drives up the margin	• Focused distribution by understanding the supplier and customer location and corresponding channels • Responsive distribution

Chart 5.4 SCS Examples

These are not the only types of segmentation, but they are the most common for optimizing the Supply Chain and we will take a closer look at them in this chapter.

In Chart 5.4, we see SCS described as a holistic solution of the above three types of segmentation structures. These address the margin, consumption velocity, customer tiering, and demand. They provide the appropriate allocation of each resource's talent into the right places, improving the bottom line and increasing the overall market share by deciding the agile or responsive Supply Chain strategy for appropriate situations.

SCS can be achieved with the combination of one or more of the segmentation structures listed previously (also described in Chart 5.4). We will look at how these structures are defined as we work our way through the examples listed in this book. Chart 5.4 adds additional explanation and depth to the three different segmentation structures we are considering.

Now that we understand some of the segmentation structures, how they work, what their objectives are, and what their focus is, we will now look at some specific examples of benefits that have been achieved through SCS.* Businesses are now slowly realizing that the SCS is critical for the simultaneous delivery of cost leadership and differentiation by offering substantial benefits. In Chart 5.5, we see a list of the areas

---

* These numbers are taken from the results attained by Chris Gordon.

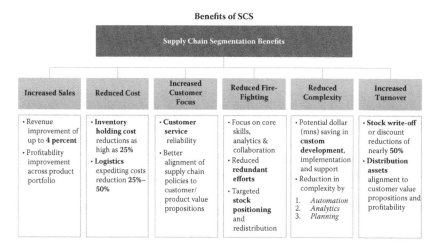

Chart 5.5 SCS Benefits

where SCS benefits have been attained and what form that benefit has taken.

The Structure of SCS

As we work our way through this book, we will consider a segmentation exercise in three different stages. These stages are:

- Analyze
- Build
- Execute

Each stage is critical to the overall process. In this chapter, we will consider the Analyze stage and in the following chapters we will consider the other two stages. In the Analyze stage, we are conceptually building the structure for SCS. The creative juices need to be engaged here as we develop a model that we will be using for the Build and Execute stages of this exercise.

In the Build stage, we will be taking the information gained in the Analyze stage and we will be testing it against actual data. We are confirming that the model that we built in the earlier Analyze stage performs as expected and desired.

In the last stage, the Execute stage, we are using SCS on a day-by-day basis to optimize the process in question. This is where we achieve actual performance improvements.

Creating an Example of SCS

In this chapter, we are going to go through a detailed segmentation/analytics example focusing on the Analyze stage of SCS. In reality, the example we are building is a demonstration of the segmentation efforts of three different companies combined into one storyline. All three of these companies were trying to solve different Supply Chain problems. Let us start by describing the three different companies and discussing the problems they were trying to solve. Then we will work through a combined example where we execute segmentation utilizing various analytics tools.

The Companies

The first company that will be used in this example is a high-tech company that utilizes contract manufacturers (CMs) for some of the parts they sell. These CMs produce a finished product and the high-tech company rebrands this as their own product and sells it as components of their main product, which they produce themselves. Their primary product is produced in their own factories. Therefore, they have a mix of managing both produced finished goods and also managing the entire production process from raw materials through to finished goods.

In the case where they use CMs, this high-tech manufacturer struggles with Demand and Supply synchronization because they use the same SKU numbers for both Demand and Supply. In the case where they do their own manufacturing, the Supply Side SKUs are for component parts and the Demand Side SKUs are for finished goods. In this second case, the Demand Side and the Supply Side are managed independently.

However, in both cases the Demand Side forecasts define the Supply Side requirements. For this company, we need to define segmentation criteria for each of these different situations, depending on what it is that they are trying to optimize.

In the second case example with which this chapter will be working, we have an aircraft manufacturing company that does most of its own manufacturing in house. It has an extensive list of suppliers with several tiers that need to be managed. The Demand Side in this case is trivial because it only has a few companies who purchase aircraft components. The Supply Side has all the complexity and therefore all the problems. The company needs to focus its segmentation efforts here.

In the third case example, the company is a mail-order pharmacy. In this case, it buys the drugs in bulk, repackages them to satisfy prescriptions, and then ships them out to the customer. In this example, the Supply Side is fairly small and simplistic because, for example, there is only one place where the company can purchase Tylenol. However, the Demand Side is extremely complex. The company delivers drugs to very different customers with very different requirements. These customers can be hospitals, clinics, and private residences. Each of these has a completely different set of needs. Additionally, some of the drugs require refrigeration and therefore require expedited delivery. Obviously, we need to put our segmentation emphasis on the Demand Side in this example.

As you can see from these examples, we need to build numerous separate customized models to manage the segmentation process for each of these Supply Chains. There is not a one-size-fits-all solution. However, there is some commonality in the initial thought process and structure building process. We will go through this exercise first. Then we will see how the different models develop.

Goals

In any segmentation exercise, the first step is to identify the problem we are trying to solve. What is our goal or objective? The segmentation model we create needs to focus on a goal or we may end up creating something that defeats our objective. After defining the goal we need to ask, "Will Segmentation help to solve this problem?"

In the case of the first company, the high-tech company, the problem was inventory obsolescence and inventory carrying cost. Ironically, high tech is similar to the fashion industry. If the product is not available when it is hot and when the customer wants it, the customer will go somewhere else and the sale is lost. In the case of the example company we are considering, it sells the vast majority of its product during the 6 weeks before Christmas. If it does not have the product when the customer comes to the store, it loses the sale. Backordering does not work because the product has to be available for Christmas. On the other hand, if it overbuilds, it has enormous obsolescence costs. By the following year, there will be technological advances and the customer will be looking for something that is bigger and better. Therefore, the optimization and management of inventory can make or break its profitability. That is the problem (goal) it was focused on solving.

For the second company, the aircraft parts manufacturer, the problem it needed to solve was supplier reliability and consistency. Suppliers had to go through a "first article" certification process for each part they produced. This meant that the first time they produced a particular part it had to go through a series of stringent tests before it could be installed on an airplane. This process takes months. In the aircraft parts manufacturing business sector, changing suppliers is quite complex. You cannot swap out suppliers at the last minute. If you have an unreliable supplier, it could shut down the production lines. The manufacturer is left with no alternative but to wait, which can be extremely expensive. Depending on the part being supplied, this could have serious consequences. However, not all parts are critical and some parts have a different level of importance from the others. Supplier consistency and reliability are critical. In this case, supplier segmentation was dependent on criteria like supplier reliability and consistency, the location of the supplier, and the product being supplied.

In the case of our third company, the mail-order pharmacy, we have a situation where it was currently shipping all

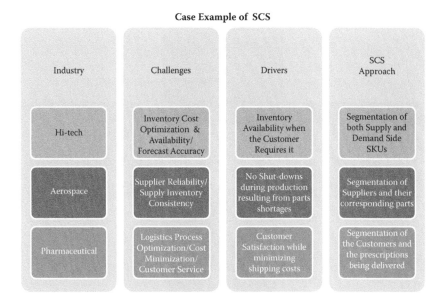

Chart 5.6 SCS Case Examples

prescriptions using FedEx and its shipping costs were enormous. Some products were critical and required FedEx overnight. However, other products, like prescription refills that were sent to private residences, were not critical and could have been delivered in numerous other less-expensive ways. For this company, the goal behind using segmentation was focused on shipping cost reductions.

Chart 5.6 summarizes what we know thus far about the characteristics of the three cases that we will be analyzing in this chapter.

Building Out the SCS Approach

Supply Chain segmentation refutes the concept of a "one size fits all" approach. It recognizes that different product types or customer groups need alternative strategies in order to achieve the maximum value. The various "segments" are designed based on the characteristics of the individual product type, customers, channels, and overall organization goal.

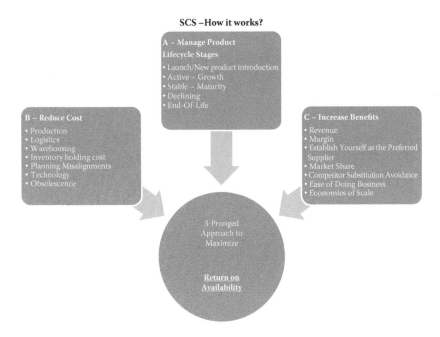

SCS –How it works?

A – Manage Product Lifecycle Stages
• Launch/New product introduction
• Active – Growth
• Stable – Maturity
• Declining
• End-Of-Life

B – Reduce Cost
• Production
• Logistics
• Warehousing
• Inventory holding cost
• Planning Misalignments
• Technology
• Obsolescence

C – Increase Benefits
• Revenue
• Margin
• Establish Yourself as the Preferred Supplier
• Market Share
• Competitor Substitution Avoidance
• Ease of Doing Business
• Economies of Scale

3-Pronged Approach to Maximize

Return on Availability

Chart 5.7 How SCS Works

SCS segments and strategies are designed to maximize the Return on Availability to the customers. Return on Availability is defined as "identifying the costs and value of making products 'available' to customers." This differs greatly based on a variety of attributes not necessarily aligned with product categories.

In Chart 5.7, we graphically see that SCS is built out based on a three-pronged approach. These three dimensions are analyzed as we focus on identifying what segmentation structure would be the best for our organization. The three prongs are:

A. Manage Products. In this prong, we are looking at the product itself. We consider its lifecycle stage and what the impact that stage has on customer service, financial measures like margins and revenue, and operational metrics like inventory management, obsolescence, planning and scheduling, etc. We will see how these considerations would be important to our high-tech and aerospace case examples as we move forward.

B. Reduce Costs. In this segment, we consider the various cost effects on the organization. For example, logistics costs are important to the pharmacy example we will be considering. Other costs, like inventory holding cost, are extremely important to our aerospace and high-tech example. Obsolescence costs are of concern to our high-tech and pharmacy examples.

C. Increase Benefits. In this segment, we look at increasing sales and market share. We also consider market accessibility and ease of customer access to our services. This category is extremely important to our high-tech example where the retailer is the critical way of distributing its products. It is of lesser importance but still has some level of importance to our pharmacy example.

Next, we will consider how each of these segments is identified and developed. We start with Category A of Chart 5.7 and build it out in Chart 5.8. Here we consider the various lifecycle stages of a product. In this simplistic example, there are three lifecycle stages. The early stage of product launch (introduction phase) is where we have very little predictive information about the product and where forecasting is challenging. We generally

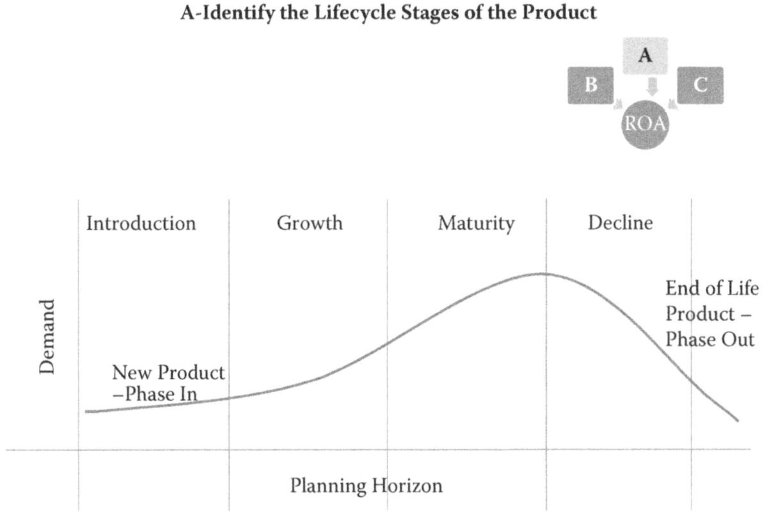

Chart 5.8 Lifecycle Stages

use tools like S&OP (discussed briefly in the last chapter) to develop some type of estimate of the anticipated product's sales performance. However, there are other problems with this product. For example, the demand is variable and inconsistent, which makes forecasting challenging. Therefore, one of the characteristics we will need to consider is inventory stability. Inventory is generally overstocked in hopes of a surge in demand. Desired customer service level is high because we want to be responsive to this anticipated surge. Safety stock is high to buffer demand variability. Margins are very high early in the product lifecycle, which compensates for some of the excess inventory stocking we tend to do. This is a critical area for the use of analytics tools, especially for the high-tech example that we are working through.

Moving forward to the active lifecycle stage (growth and maturity phases), this is where we have a stable market for the product. Volume variability is at its minimum and is reasonably predictable. High customer service is easy to attain at minimal inventory levels. Margins are still strong. This is the lifecycle stage where the product is a cash cow for our organization. These considerations are critical for both our aerospace and high-tech examples.

As we move forward, we move toward the EOL stage (decline phase) of our product. We have declining and often intermittent demand. Inventory planning is critical because we run the risk of becoming overwhelmed with obsolete inventories. Margins are at a minimum. Customer service levels are declining because we often do not care about how much we sell of this product. The organization is looking forward to its new product that is replacing this old and obsolete product. The cost of maintaining inventory and service levels for this product is often more than the margins earned. Because of all these negative reasons, a planning system that focuses on product "burn out" becomes important. We do not want any safety stock. We want to make the product a "make to order" product where we only build it when we have an order for it. We are not interested in a fast and efficient channel and optimal Supply Chain support. We look for the cheapest support structure possible when we consider the delivery of this product. All three of our case example organizations would need to have help in this area.

As described in Chart 5.8, the analytics component in this product type is critical for all three lifecycle stages. In addition, we will see the applications of these analytics tools as we move forward with our SCS example later in this book. Supply Chain considerations that affect the various stages include (this was also stressed in the previous chapter on analytics):

- Launch/New Product Introduction (NPI)—During this stage, high uncertainties exist in demand trend, pricing, competition, service level, etc., which requires extensive use of analytics to understand and build the Supply Chain. This stage requires the most intensive monitoring by the product planners.
- Active/Growth Stage and Stable/Maturity Stage—These stages are where we introduce automation. They become stable stages where process cycles and demands are somewhat repetitive and therefore predictable. Firms utilize ERP and other applications to efficiently manage the Supply Chain including forecasting and inventory optimization for lowest cost of service. These tend to be the stages that require the least amount of product planner involvement.
- Declining and EOL Stages—During these last stages of the product lifecycle we encounter declining demand. We need to respond by repurposing and redeploying capacity and inventory. This stage is where product planners once again become involved in order to strategically avoid a buildup of obsolete inventory.

Moving on to Category B of Chart 5.7, we take a closer look at cost drivers and their affect on the Return on Availability in Chart 5.9. These drivers may or may not apply. We need to look at the ones that apply and consider their impact. From that, we derive corresponding attributes. Reviewing the attributes in which we are interested, we need to come up with corresponding Cost of Availability (COA) considerations (at the bottom of Chart 5.9).

COA can be estimated by analyzing the Supply Chain parameters that have a direct impact on the product, Supply Chain, and service cost. In Chart 5.9, we see an example of

B-Identify cost drivers that impact return on availability

Cost Drivers	Impact of the Driver	Attributes		
Lifecycle Length	Product availability/obsolesence	Long	Medium	Short
Volatility	Level of inventory buffering	Low	Medium	High
Product Customization	Interdependencies/stock outs	Low	Medium	High
Product Criticality	Customer operational shutdowns	Low	Medium	High
Geography/Location	Pipeline length/inventory staging	Onshore	Nearshore	Farshore
Product Turnaround	Shelf life/inventory levels	Fast	Medium	Slow
Gross Margin	Risk/profitability	High	Medium	Low
Seasonality	Inventory buildup/planning	Heavy	Medium	None
Channel Hazards	Planning/inventory costs	High	Medium	Low

Cost of Availability		
High	Medium	Low

Minimize Cost

Chart 5.9 Cost Drivers

various cost components. This list may not be complete for your specific business sector and other drivers may need to be added to this chart. We then use this chart as our example, selecting from the numerous cost attributes and their corresponding impact on the overall segmentation analysis process.

Moving on to Category C in Chart 5.7, we counterbalance the cost considerations with benefits. In Chart 5.10, we look at customers categorized into three tiers based on their strategic significance to the business operation. The Customer Segments category defines the benefits that would be made available to different segments through Supply Chain. It defines the support structure that would be the most beneficial for each of these segments. The value attained by supporting each tier is very different. Hence, tiering determines the level of service and the internal planning and support structure that the organization needs to construct.

At this point, we turn to analytics. We consider each of the three categories of segmentation and create a three-dimensional analysis of these categories, and through the data, we build

C -Identify the customer segments that drive benefits

Segments	Definition
Tier-1	High-priority customers with strategic/critical importance to our company (The 20% of the customers that make up 80% of our business)
Tier-2	Medium priority customers who deserve the next best level of Supply Chain support
Tier-3	Low-priority customers who are relatively at the lowest level in the hierarchy (The majority of our customers, around 50 to 60%, who make up only about 20% of our business)

Chart 5.10 Customer Segments

out our three-dimensional segmentation matrix. We follow these steps in this process:

1. Collect the necessary data for each of the three catego-ries A, B, and C as seen in Chart 5.11.
2. Analyze the data in each of these categories to deter-mine Return on Availability and cluster this into Supply Chain segments by building out the three-dimensional matrix as seen in Chart 5.12.
3. Aggregate similar segments for the entire organization to come up with a manageable number of segments (10 or fewer) as shown in Chart 5.13.
4. Deploy the necessary Supply Chain design based on the following segments:

   - Product availability (service level) to the customers
   - Lead time to different customers
   - Supply Chain business model

In the example of Chart 5.12, which is a revision of Chart 5.7, the process is kept simplistic by allowing only three alterna-tives for each Category. For A, only three lifecycle stages are allowed, but in reality you will probably have twice that many

Segmentation Tailored to Your Key Business Drivers

Cost Drivers	Impact of the Driver	Attribute Impact	
		Low	High
Lifecycle Length	Product availability/obsolesence		■
Volatility	Level of inventory buffering		■
Product Customization	Interdependencies/stock outs		■
Product Criticality	Customer operational shutdowns		■
Geography/Location	Pipeline length/inventory staging		■
Product Turnaround	Shelf life/inventory levels		■
Gross Margin	Risk/profitability		■
Seasonality	Inventory buildup/planning		■
Channel Hazards	Planning/inventory costs	■	

Chart 5.11 Segmentation Tailored to Business Drivers

Process to determine the SC Segments to
maximize return on availability

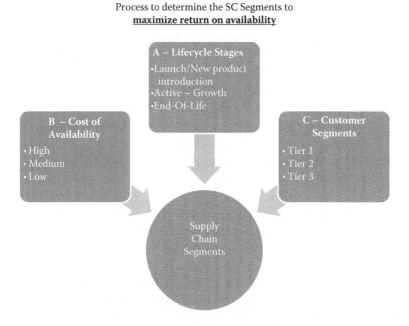

Chart 5.12 Maximize ROA

Example–Segmentation Matrix to
maximize return on availability (A)

Lifecycle Stage	Cost of Availability	Tier 1 Customers			Tier 2 Customers			Tier 3 Customers		
Launch	Low									
	Med									
	High									
Active	Low									
	Med									
	High									
End of Life	Low									
	Med									
	High									

Chart 5.13 Example—Maximize ROA (A)

stages. Similarly, for Category B only three attributes for COA (see Chart 5.9) are shown, but in reality you may experience many more stages. For example, the Business Attributes may be more along a continuum, as seen in Chart 5.11, making segmentation more complex.

Also for Category C, you may have more than three customer tiers. For the example here, I am only using three stages in order to keep the example set small, as can be seen in the graphic of Chart 5.12. Similarly, Category C could be supplier tiers if we are focused on the Supply Side as opposed to the Demand Side of segmentation, which we will see in the aircraft parts example. However, you will possibly want to expand on one or more of the stages when you get ready to build your own model.

The next step in this process is the construction of the segmentation matrix. I will walk you through this process over a series of charts. It will give you a more thorough and complete understanding of the objectives and purpose of the segmentation matrix. In the end, this process defines the segments and establishes the foundation for the decision logic flow, which is critical when we build the model that will segment out your

Example –Segmentation Matrix to
maximize return on availability (B)

Lifecycle Stage	Cost of Availability	Tier 1 Customers			Tier 2 Customers			Tier 3 Customers		
		Availability	Lead Time	SC Business Model	Availability	Lead Time	SC Business Model	Availability	Lead Time	SC Business Model
Launch	Low									
	Med									
	High									
Active	Low									
	Med									
	High									
End of Life	Low									
	Med									
	High									

Chart 5.14 Example—Maximize ROA (B)

customers, suppliers, and products. The first step is to visualize all the different dimensions with which we are dealing. In Chart 5.13, we see the three dimensions and the subcategories associated with each of the dimensions. The three Tiers for Customers are listed across the top. On the left are the three lifecycle stages. Sub to the lifecycle stages are the COA levels of high, medium, and low.

Next, we will take Chart 5.13 and Supply Chain subcategories. This can be seen in Chart 5.14. For our example, we have elected to subcategorize each of our dimensions with expectations about availability, lead time, and specifically what type of business model we are expecting to execute. Within each of these subcategories we will need to indicate our expectations and priorities for that specific dimension.

By way of definition, the different types of Supply Chain business models we will be using in this example can be defined as follows (recognize that even these definitions may need to be customized for your particular segmentation project).

Efficient Supply Chain—In this case, we would design a Supply Chain that would provide the desired service level to the customer with minimum Supply Chain cost. Key elements of this Supply Chain include:

- Extensive use of ERP and planning tools to automate the planning and scheduling processes
- Design a "low touch" process that requires minimum planner intervention
- Focus on reducing Supply Chain cost and use tools like Inventory Optimization to optimize working capital

Agile Supply Chain—For this, we design a Supply Chain that would be agile, flexible, and responsive. Key elements of this Supply Chain are:

- Invest in resources to collect market information
- Use "advance forecast/predictive analytics" to understand historical data and sense the change in the market
- Focus on flexible design that can respond to the changing needs in the area of capacity and lead time
- Prioritize on velocity to rapidly respond to changing market conditions
- Invest in collaboration platforms to share forecast, order, and inventory information across all trading partners in the Supply Chain

Custom Supply Chain—Design the Supply Chain to support unique requirements specific to product, customer, and market dynamics. Key elements of this type of Supply Chain are:

- Poor data available making it hard to predict future trends
- Poor stability in the transaction history and performance
- Normally supported by some form of an S&OP process

Moving forward in our example, we will next look at how each of the dimensions is filled in. In Chart 5.15, we see the finalized construction of the matrix. As already noted, across the top we see one dimension, which is customer tiers. Down the left-hand side we see the other two dimensions of lifecycle

Example–Segmentation Matrix to
maximize return on availability (C)

Lifecycle Stage	Cost of Availability	Tier 1 Customers			Tier 2 Customers			Tier 3 Customers		
		Availability	Lead Time	SC Business Model	Availability	Lead Time	SC Business Model	Availability	Lead Time	SC Business Model
Launch	Low	High	5 Days	Custom	Medium	25 Days	Agile	Medium	30 Days	Agile
	Med	High	5 Days	Custom	Medium	30 Days	Agile	Low	35 Days	Efficient
	High	High	5 Days	Custom	Medium	35 Days	Efficient	Low	40 Days	Efficient
Active	Low	High	10 Days	Efficient	High	25 Days	Efficient	High	30 Days	Efficient
	Med	High	10 Days	Efficient	High	25 Days	Efficient	Medium	30 Days	Efficient
	High	High	30 Days	Agile	Medium	30 Days	Efficient	Low	35 Days	Efficient
End of Life	Low	High	15 Days	Efficient	Medium	35 Days	Efficient	Low	40 Days	Efficient
	Med	High	35 Days	Agile	Low	40 Days	Efficient	Low	45 Days	Efficient
	High	High	40 Days	Agile	Low	45 Days	Efficient	Low	50 Days	Efficient

Chart 5.15 Example—Maximize ROA (C-1)

stage and COA. Within each lifecycle stage, we see the three COA alternatives. Therefore, if we read the matrix we see all three dimensions graphed in this two-dimensional format. For example, if we read the highlighted box in the upper left-hand corner of the matrix in Chart 5.15 we see an example where we have (1) a Tier 1 Customer, (2) a lifecycle stage of Launch, and (3) a COA of Medium.

From our data, we learn that for the intersection of these three dimensions we need the following (this is information we fill in and which is critical for the next stage of the process):

1. High availability to the customer, which means a high service level
2. A lead time of 5 days, which requires us to be extremely responsive
3. A Supply Chain Business Model of Customized, which generally means S&OP

For a second example, if we read the highlighted box in the lower right-hand corner of the matrix in Chart 5.15, we see an example where we have (1) a Tier 3 Customer, (2) a lifecycle stage of Active, and (3) a COA of High.

From our data, we determine that for these three dimensions we need to input the following values into our matrix:

1. Low availability for the customer, which means a low service level
2. A long lead time of 35 days
3. A Supply Chain Business Model of Efficient, which generally means no buffer inventory and a focus on BTO (Build to Order)

Based on different values of the three categories (our three dimensions—lifecycle stages, Return on Availability, and customer), we would end up with 27 (3 lifecycle stages × 3 Return on Availability options × 3 customer tiers) unique Supply Chain segments. This is too large a number to manage realistically. We need to logically group these in ways that would minimize the operational processes.

Chart 5.16 takes Chart 5.15 and creates logical groups based on the operational complexity and the Supply Chain considerations of each of the processes. Two examples of these types of groupings are highlighted in Chart 5.16 (upper left-hand corner and lower right-hand corner). In this way, we build Supply Chain operational structures that would have similar process methodologies. After aggregation and consolidation, most organizations are able to get down to anywhere between 6 and 10 unique segments.

In the example of Chart 5.17, we took Chart 5.16 and grouped all 27 three-dimensional intersections. The groupings were made logically based on the Supply Chain characteristics that we were mapping, which in this example were specifically focused on:

• Availability
• Lead Time
• Supply Chain Business Model

In the end, we ended up with six logical segments. Different individuals may have grouped them differently. The real test

Example–Segmentation Matrix to
maximize return on availability (C)

Lifecycle Stage	Cost of Availability	Tier 1 Customers			Tier 2 Customers			Tier 3 Customers		
		Availability	Lead Time	SC Business Model	Availability	Lead Time	SC Business Model	Availability	Lead Time	SC Business Model
Launch	Low	High	5 Days	Custom	Medium	25 Days	Agile	Medium	30 Days	Agile
Launch	Med	High	5 Days	Custom	Medium	30 Days	Agile	Low	35 Days	Efficient
Launch	High	High	5 Days	Custom	Medium	35 Days	Efficient	Low	40 Days	Efficient
Active	Low	High	10 Days	Efficient	High	25 Days	Efficient	High	30 Days	Efficient
Active	Med	High	10 Days	Efficient	High	25 Days	Efficient	Medium	30 Days	Efficient
Active	High	High	30 Days	Agile	Medium	30 Days	Efficient	Low	35 Days	Efficient
End of Life	Low	High	15 Days	Efficient	Medium	35 Days	Efficient	Low	40 Days	Efficient
End of Life	Med	High	35 Days	Agile	Low	40 Days	Efficient	Low	45 Days	Efficient
End of Life	High	High	40 Days	Agile	Low	45 Days	Efficient	Low	50 Days	Efficient

Chart 5.16   Example—Maximize ROA (C-2)

Example–Segmentation Matrix to
maximize return on availability (C)

Lifecycle Stage	Cost of Availability	Tier 1 Customers			Tier 2 Customers			Tier 3 Customers		
		Availability	Lead Time	SC Business Model	Availability	Lead Time	SC Business Model	Availability	Lead Time	SC Business Model
Launch	Low		[1]		Medium	25 Days	Agile	Medium	30 Days	Agile
Launch	Med	High	5 Days	Custom	Medium	30 Days	Agile		[6]	
Launch	High				Medium	35 Days	Efficient	Low	40 Days	Efficient
Active	Low	High	10 Days	Efficient	[2]			High	30 Days	Efficient
Active	Med				High	25 Days	Efficient	Medium	30 Days	Efficient
Active	High	High	[3] 30 Days	Agile	Medium	30 Days	Efficient		[6]	
End of Life	Low	High	[2] 15 Days	Efficient	Medium	35 Days	Efficient	Low	40 Days	Efficient
End of Life	Med	[3]								
End of Life	High	High	35 Days	Agile						

Chart 5.17   Example—Maximize ROA (C-3)

Example – Service level Segmentation, rationalized and simplified into 6 unique segments

Lifecycle Stage	Cost of Availability	Tier 1 Customers			Tier 2 Customers			Tier 3 Customers		
		Availability	Lead Time	SC Business Model	Availability	Lead Time	SC Business Model	Availability	Lead Time	SC Business Model
Launch	Low				Medium	25 Days	Agile (4)			
Launch	Med	High (1)	5 Days	Custom						
Launch	High									
Active	Low	High	25 Days	Efficient (2)						
Active	Med									
Active	High				Medium (5)	30 Days	Efficient			
End of Life	Low							Low (6)	40 Days	Efficient
End of Life	Med	High	35 Days (3)	Agile						
End of Life	High									

Chart 5.18 Example—Broken into Segments

is in the execution of this model and we see how products in each of the 27 dimensional quadrants perform. If they do not perform as desired, we may have to adjust our segmentation structure to create something that is more desirable and which gives us the results we defined early on as our goals.

Moving forward, in Chart 5.18 we see how logical groups are created and where some values, like lead time, are averaged or taken at their minimum for the group. For example, in Chart 5.18 for Segment 1 we see that this segment requires high availability with short lead time. This segment would have high margins. It has the new products that are being introduced (NPI—New Product Introduction) to the market and they require a high level of service and attention. However, this segment has poor predictive data so it would require a customized Supply Chain Business Model. Specifically, for Segment 1 we would require the implementation of S&OP for the forecasting, planning, and scheduling process.

Looking at another example in Chart 5.18, we see Segment 6 where we require low product availability. This is the other extreme end of the product lifecycle where we are focused on the EOL products. Lead time is at its highest and the Supply

Chain Business Model is efficient. This means that we are looking for a methodology that offers us minimal inventories. We are looking at BTO products and not keeping any inventory on the product.

At this point, we should feel successful because we have defined our segments. However, this is rarely the final segmentation solution. It is just the first step in the process. Often, as we test out our segmentation approach we will find things that just do not make sense and we will need to modify our structure. However, that is okay. It is a normal part of the development process. This process is iterative and I have known companies that are still making tweaks and adjustments after having run their model for years.

The next steps in the SCS process are heavily ingrained with analytics. It is an even bigger effort than the one we have already completed. We start by going through a data cleansing process, and then we test our segmentation structure using the analytics models we develop. However, we will discuss all of that later in this chapter. At this point, it would be a good idea to catch up with our three case examples.

Returning to Our Three Case Example Companies

Before we get too far ahead of ourselves in the segmentation process, let us catch up with our example companies, and see how each of them created an appropriate segmentation structure for themselves. I will not be revealing anything specific about any of these companies because most companies appropriately see their segmentation structure as a confidential strategic tool. What I will be sharing is the thought process that they needed to go through. The results I present here are simplified examples. The actual results were significantly more detailed.

Let us start with the easiest example and then move toward the more complex example. The first example that I will discuss is the aircraft parts manufacturer where the focus is on supplier reliability and consistency, especially in their "first article" certification process. In this case, supplier segmentation was dependent on criteria like supplier reliability and consistency, the location of the supplier, and the product being supplied. We start by reflecting back on Chart 5.7 and look closely at the Return on Availability. We need to consider the three key components of availability, which are:

A—Manage the Product Lifecycle Stages
B—Reduce Cost
C—Increase Benefits

In Chart 5.19, we see an aerospace-specific example of the analysis performed for Return on Availability. In the lifecycle stages (A), First Article processes are highlighted as a specific stage because they require a unique set of lead times, inventory planning, and throughput scheduling. For cost (B), we see costs that are specific to Supply Side cost minimization. For example, Kanbans and Vendor Managed Inventories (VMI)

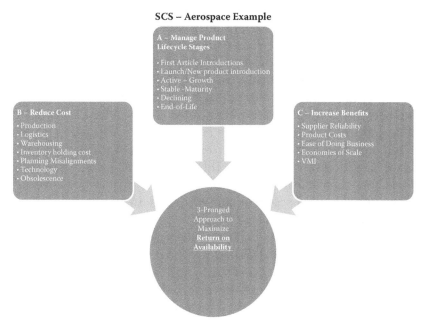

Chart 5.19 SCS—Aerospace Example

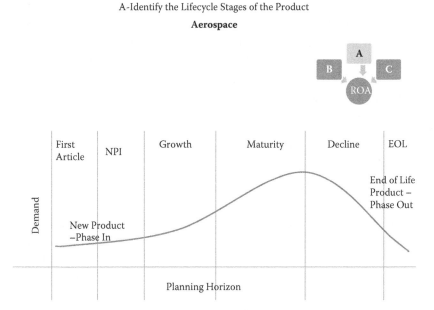

Chart 5.20 Aerospace Lifecycle Stages

can reduce and defer a lot of the cost of raw materials (received materials). Continuing in our aerospace example looking at the benefits of the model, we specifically look at suppliers rather than customers. We are interested in seeing what benefits can be achieved by segmenting the Supply Side of the equation.

Moving forward in our analysis of Return on Availability, we see the aerospace lifecycle stages (stage A in Chart 5.19) detailed in Chart 5.20. In this case, we have six stages. Since I did not want to present an enormous spreadsheet in this book, I will lump the stages into pairs putting the first two together, then the middle two, and then last two. However, when working this SCS model we need to break out all six stages separately.

Next, we look at the corresponding graphic for Chart 5.19, stage B, and we see it detailed in Chart 5.21. We use the cost drivers identified in Chart 5.19 and analyze each of them individually. We use these drivers to define what is meant by High, Medium, or Low COA. The impact of each of these drivers helps us in determining the Supply Chain Impact that is eventually built out in Chart 5.24.

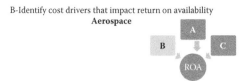

B-Identify cost drivers that impact return on availability
Aerospace

Cost Drivers	Impact of the Driver	Attributes		
Production	Shutdown because of missing parts	High	Medium	Small
Logistics	Responsive vs Cost Minimized	Low	Medium	High
Warehousing	Accessibility/Availability	Low	Medium	High
Inventory Holding Cost	Overstock vs Stock outs	Low	Medium	High
Planning Misalignments	Right Product at right time	Low	Medium	High
Technology	Data tracking/Event Management	Low	Medium	High
Obsolescence	Write off risk	High	Medium	Low

Chart 5.21 Aerospace Cost Drivers

C-Identify the supplier segments that drive benefits
Aerospace

Segments	Definition
Tier-1	Suppliers that supply critical production items with risk of production shutdown–products with long first article processing lead time
Tier-2	Medium priority suppliers with critical parts but where we have alternative certified suppliers
Tier-3	Low priority suppliers with non-critical parts and numerous alternative suppliers

Chart 5.22 Aerospace Supplier Segments

Last, we look at stage C from Chart 5.19, which is detailed in Chart 5.22. Here we see the tiering of the suppliers. Again, we are keeping this example simplistic, but it is easy to see where there may be more than three tiers because in reality there are more than three different groupings of suppliers.

Process to determine the SC Segments to
maximize return on availability-Aerospace

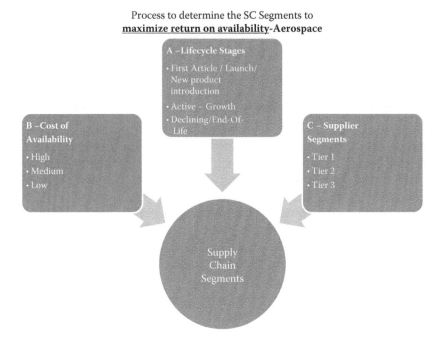

Chart 5.23 Aerospace ROA

The information from Charts 5.20, 5.21, and 5.22 is integrated into Chart 5.23, and then detailed in Chart 5.24.

Looking more closely at Chart 5.24, we see the same structure that we saw in Chart 5.15. What is unique to aerospace is that the tiering across the top is focused on suppliers, and the Supply Chain characteristics on which we are focusing are supplier specific; for this example they are as follows:

- Criticality—How critical is the on-time arrival and availability of this part to the production process? Will this shut down production? Are we hampered by only having one or a limited number of suppliers of this component? Are alternative suppliers hard to find?
- Lead Time—What is the allowable lead time for this part?
- Supply Chain Business Model—For the sake of simplicity, we are using the same three business models that were described earlier: Custom, Agile, and Efficient. More business models are available and could have

Example –Segmentation Matrix to
maximize return on availability-Aerospace

Lifecycle Stage	Cost of Availability	Tier 1 Suppliers			Tier 2 Suppliers			Tier 3 Suppliers		
		Criticality	Lead Time	SC Business Model	Criticality	Lead Time	SC Business Model	Criticality	Lead Time	SC Business Model
Launch	Low	High	120 Days	Custom	Medium	120 Days	Efficient	Medium	120 Days	Efficient
Launch	Med	High	120 Days	Custom	Medium	120 Days	Efficient	Low	120 Days	Efficient
Launch	High	High	120 Days	Custom	Medium	120 Days	Efficient	Low	120 Days	Efficient
Active	Low	High	10 Days	Efficient	High	20 Days	Efficient	Low	30 Days	Efficient
Active	Med	High	10 Days	Agile	High	20 Days	Efficient	Medium	30 Days	Efficient
Active	High	High	10 Days	Agile	Medium	20 Days	Agile	Low	30 Days	Efficient
End of Life	Low	High	20 Days	Efficient	Low	30 Days	Efficient	Low	40 Days	Efficient
End of Life	Med	High	30 Days	Efficient	Low	40 Days	Efficient	Low	45 Days	Efficient
End of Life	High	High	40 Days	Efficient	Low	50 Days	Efficient	Low	50 Days	Efficient

Chart 5.24 Aerospace Initial Segmentation Matrix

been utilized. We will learn more about the different business/planning/scheduling models/options in a later chapter.

Using the information from the three dimensions, we analyze each quadrant of the table and fill in the Supply Chain characteristics that will optimize this quadrant. For example, for Tier 1 suppliers that are producing products that are in the "Launch" lifecycle stage, and which have low COA, we are indicating that the Supply Chain characteristics would classify this quadrant as follows:

- Criticality is High
- Lead time is long—120 days
- The SC Business Model is custom—S&OP

We proceed to identify this quadrant information for each of the three-dimensional quadrants in Chart 5.24. Finally, we are ready to take Chart 5.24 and use it to generate the segmentation groupings that can be seen in Chart 5.25.

Example–Segmentation Matrix to
maximize return on availability-Aerospace

Lifecycle Stage	Cost of Availability	Tier 1 Suppliers			Tier 2 Suppliers			Tier 3 Suppliers		
		Criticality	Lead Time	SC Business Model	Criticality	Lead Time	SC Business Model	Criticality	Lead Time	SC Business Model
Launch	Low	High	120 Days	Custom	Medium	120 Days	Efficient	Medium	120 Days	Efficient
	Med	High	120 Days	Custom	Medium	120 Days	Efficient	Low	120 Days	Efficient
	High	High	120 Days	Custom	Medium	120Days	Efficient	Low	120 Days	Efficient
Active	Low	High	10 Days	Efficient	High	20 Days	Efficient	Low	40 Days	Efficient
	Med	High	10 Days	Agile	High	20 Days	Efficient	Medium	30 Days	Efficient
	High	High	10 Days	Agile	Medium	20 Days	Agile	Low	30 Days	Efficient
End of Life	Low	High	20 Days	Efficient	Low	30 Days	Efficient	Low	40 Days	Efficient
	Med	High	30 Days	Efficient	Low	40 Days	Efficient	Low	15 Days	Efficient
	High	High	40 Days	Efficient	Low	50 Days	Efficient	Low	50 Days	Efficient

Chart 5.25 Aerospace Broken into Segments

At this point, we are current with our aerospace example. We have caught up to where we need to be in this chapter and we are ready to move this example to the next chapter. However, before we do that we need to catch up with our other two case examples as well. In order to simplify the process, I will only focus on the differences between these other examples and what we have already seen in this chapter.

For the pharmaceutical example, we again start with the COA stages as diagramed in Chart 5.26. Since the focus is on reducing delivery costs based on customer segmentation, we can see that in this example the lifecycle stages will play a minor and almost insignificant role, and that the major focus will be on shipping cost reductions while at the same time meeting customer delivery requirements.

Moving forward, we build out Chart 5.27 where we have a simplistic example of the product lifecycle stages, the COA (which is focused on delivery costs), and the customer segmentation to maximize customer satisfaction and customer benefits.

Next, we build out the Return on Availability matrix, as shown in Chart 5.28. Here we see the three customer tiers, the

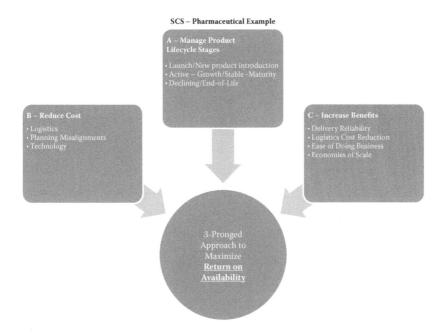

Chart 5.26 SCS—Pharmaceutical Example

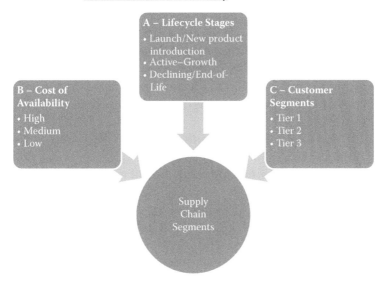

Chart 5.27 Pharmaceutical ROA

Example –Segmentation Matrix to
maximize return on availability-Pharmaceutical

Lifecycle Stage	Cost of Availability	Tier 1 Customer			Tier 2 Customer			Tier 3 Customer		
		Shipping Criticality	Lead Time	SC Business Model	Shipping Criticality	Lead Time	SC Business Model	Shipping Criticality	Lead Time	SC Business Model
Launch	Low	Low	2 Days	Custom	Low	2 Days	Efficient	Low	3 Days	Efficient
	Med	Medium	2 Days	Custom	Medium	2 Days	Efficient	Medium	3 Days	Efficient
	High	High	1 Day	Custom	High	1 Day	Efficient	High	1 Day	Efficient
Active	Low	Low	2 Days	Efficient	Low	2 Days	Efficient	Low	3 Days	Efficient
	Med	Medium	2 Days	Efficient	Medium	2 Days	Efficient	Medium	3 Days	Efficient
	High	High	1 Day	Efficient	High	1 Day	Efficient	High	1 Day	Efficient
End of Life	Low	Low	2 Days	Efficient	Low	2 Days	Efficient	Low	3 Days	Efficient
	Med	Medium	2 Days	Efficient	Medium	2 Days	Efficient	Medium	3 Days	Efficient
	High	High	1 Day	Efficient	High	1 Day	Efficient	High	1 Day	Efficient

Chart 5.28 Pharmaceutical Initial Segmentation Matrix

COA stages, and the lifecycle stages as defined in Chart 5.27. We also look at three examples of Supply Chain characteristics, which in this case are as follows:

Shipping Criticality—How critical is it that the product arrives on time? Is there a refrigeration requirement that goes with this product that will in turn make shipping critical? Is this a new prescription requiring urgent delivery, or is this a refill prescription that is not as urgent?

Lead Time—How much time do we have to deliver the product?

Supply Chain Business Model—Same definitions as previously used.

With the matrix of Chart 5.28 filled out and with the Supply Chain characteristics mapped into each quadrant, we are ready to define the segments that will be utilized to optimize Supply Chain logistics planning. The results are the four segments that can be seen in Chart 5.29. The focus in

Example – Segmentation Matrix to
maximize return on availability-**Pharmaceutical**

Lifecycle Stage	Cost of Availability	Tier 1 Customer			Tier 2 Customer			Tier 3 Customer		
		Shipping Criticality	Lead Time	SC Business Model	Shipping Criticality	Lead Time	SC Business Model	Shipping Criticality	Lead Time	SC Business Model
Launch	Low	Low	2 Days	Custom	Low	2 Days	Efficient	Low	3 Days	Efficient
	Med	Medium 1	2 Days	Custom	Medium	2 Days	Efficient	Medium 4	3 Days	Efficient
	High	High	1 Day	Custom	High	1 Day	Efficient	High	1 Day	Efficient
Active	Low	Low	2 Days	Efficient	Low	2 Days	Efficient	Low	3 Days	Efficient
	Med	Medium	2 Days 2	Efficient	Medium	2 Days	Efficient	Medium	3 Days	Efficient
	High	High	1 Day 3	Efficient	High	1 Day	Efficient	High	1 Day	Efficient
End of Life	Low	Low	2 Days	Efficient	Low	2 Days	Efficient	Low	3 Days	Efficient
	Med	Medium	2 Days	Efficient	Medium	2 Days	Efficient	Medium	3 Days	Efficient
	High	High	1 Day	Efficient	High	1 Day	Efficient	High	1 Day	Efficient

Chart 5.29 Pharmaceutical Broken into Segments

creating these segments was on lead time and shipping criticality rather than on the Supply Chain Business Model as was the focus in the previous example. That is why the segmentation structure may seem to be defined slightly differently than previously. However, the segmentation structure should always focus on the goal, which in this case was primarily customer satisfaction and secondarily minimizing shipping costs.

Our last example brings us to the high-tech company that was trying to balance both supply and demand segmentation structures. The goal in this case was product availability at minimum inventory levels. Looking at Chart 5.30, we see that this example is significantly more complex than the previous examples. For example, the lifecycle stages (A) have a phase-out stage called BTO before the product is closed out completely. In reality, we actually ended up with five different phase-out stages for the product lifecycle of this organization. The Reduced Cost (B) stage also has significantly more elements than in the previous example. Also in the Benefits (C) stage, we identified numerous components that affect the tiering of our customer groupings.

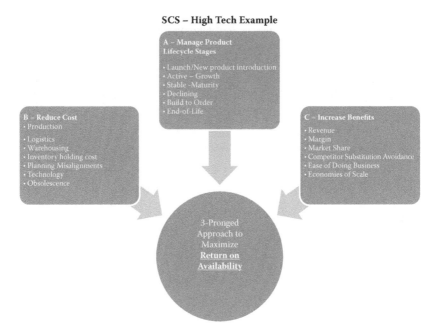

Chart 5.30 SCS—High-Tech Example

Moving on to identify the Supply Chain segments, we see Chart 5.31 where the various segments are defined. Again, in this example I have reduced the lifecycle stages to three and the customer segments to three, but in reality there were many more stages and segments that needed to be analyzed.

With the segments defined, we can now build out the matrix in Chart 5.32, again looking at an example that has three customer tiers. In this case, the customer tiers are as follows:

- Tier 1—The large consumers who purchase the majority of our product like Best Buy, Fry's, Sam's, or Costco.
- Tier 2—The large department stores like Walmart and Target.
- Tier 3—The small mall electronics outlets.

For the lifecycle stages, I have again simplified this example down to three stages but in reality, there were close to 10 stages. As we learned earlier, there were five EOL stages alone. COA is primarily focused on inventory reduction and logistics cost reduction.

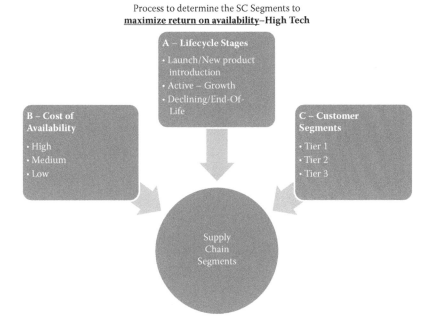

Process to determine the SC Segments to
maximize return on availability–High Tech

Chart 5.31 High-Tech ROA

Example –Segmentation Matrix to
maximize return on availability–High Tech

Lifecycle Stage	Cost of Availability	Tier 1 Customer				Tier 2 Customer				Tier 3 Customer			
		Product Availability	Safety Stock/ Inventory Buffering Levels	SC Business Model		Product Availability	Safety Stock/ Inventory Buffering Levels	SC Business Model		Product Availability	Safety Stock/ Inventory Buffering Levels	SC Business Model	
Launch	Low	High	Max	Custom		High	Max	Custom		High	Medium	Custom	
	Med	High	Max	Custom		High	Max	Custom		High	Medium	Custom	
	High	High	Max	Custom		High	Max	Custom		High	Medium	Custom	
Active	Low	High	Medium	Agile		High	Medium	Agile		High	Medium	Agile	
	Med	High	Medium	Agile		High	Medium	Agile		High	Medium	Agile	
	High	High	Medium	Agile		High	Medium	Agile		High	Medium	Agile	
End of Life	Low	Low	Minimum	Efficient		Low	Minimum	Efficient		Low	Minimum	Efficient	
	Med	Low	Minimum	Efficient		Low	Minimum	Efficient		Low	Minimum	Efficient	
	High	Low	Minimum	Efficient		Low	Minimum	Efficient		Low	Minimum	Efficient	

Chart 5.32 High-Tech Initial Segmentation Matrix

Example–Segmentation Matrix to
maximize return on availability–High Tech

Lifecycle Stage	Cost of Availability		Tier 1 Customer			Tier 2 Customer			Tier 3 Customer		
			Product Availability	Safety Stock/ Inventory Buffering Levels	SC Business Model	Product Availability	Safety Stock/ Inventory Buffering Levels	SC Business Model	Product Availability	Safety Stock/ Inventory Buffering Levels	SC Business Model
Launch	Low		High	Max	Custom	High	Max	Custom	High	Medium	Custom
	Med		High	Max	Custom	High	Max	Custom	High	Medium	Custom
	High		High	Max	Custom	High	Max	Custom	High	Medium	Custom
Active	Low		High	Medium	Agile	High	Medium	Agile	High	Medium	Agile
	Med		High	Medium	Agile	High	Medium	Agile	High	Medium	Agile
	High		High	Medium	Agile	High	Medium	Agile	High	Medium	Agile
End of Life	Low		Low	Minimum	Efficient	Low	Minimum	Efficient	Low	Minimum	Efficient
	Med		Low	Minimum	Efficient	Low	Minimum	Efficient	Low	Minimum	Efficient
	High		Low	Minimum	Efficient	Low	Minimum	Efficient	Low	Minimum	Efficient

Chart 5.33 High-Tech Broken into Segments

From Chart 5.32, we break into the segments shown in Chart 5.33. In this simplified example, there are only four segments, but when we break out all the actual lifecycle stages, we end up with double that number of segments.

At this point, we have constructed segmentation structures for a generic example and for three case examples. Now we will return to our generic process and attempt to continue our journey toward utilizing segmentation to achieve process optimization.

Driving toward SCS Execution

At this point, we have built the foundation of a segmentation structure for our organization. Now it would be good to discuss the SCS approach at a high level and look at all the steps in the approach. Then we will discuss the steps we still need to consider in order to complete our SCS exercise. Chart 5.34 presents the end-to-end holistic approach, which leverages all

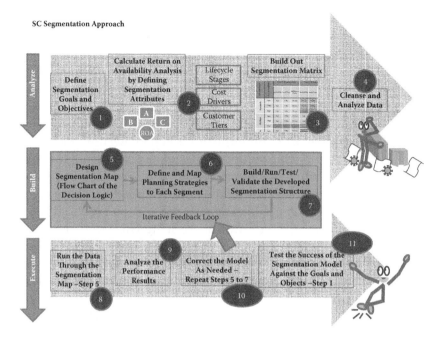

Chart 5.34 SCS Approach

three key components used to segment the Supply Chain in order to maximize the Return on Availability to customers.

The SCS approach in Chart 5.34 is broken into three major components:

- Analyze
- Build
- Execute

Up to now in this chapter, we have been focused on the Analyze process in that we focused on identifying the segments on which we will need to work. The steps in the Analyze process started with a definition of the goals and objectives of the segmentation effort (Step 1). This information is then utilized to calculate the Return on Availability (Step 2). From here, we can build a segmentation matrix (Step 3), which can be broken into specific segments that we will use in the Build and Execute stages of SCS. That is what we have accomplished up to now in this chapter. The only remaining step in the Analyze process that we still need to consider is the cleansing and analysis of the data, which will be discussed later.

The next process in the SCS approach map is the Build process, which will be discussed in detail in the next chapter. Within the Build process, we are focused on developing a logic roadmap that can be used to logically map each SKU (Stock Keeping Unit), customer, or supplier to its corresponding segment (Step 5). We start by building a logic flowchart defining the analysis that each product or customer goes through when determining in which segment it will be placed. An analytics software tool needs to be developed and, depending on its complexity, it can be executed using spreadsheet software. It may also need to be integrated into the existing ERP environment.

Step 6 defines the planning and scheduling structure that needs to be created for each segment. It uses the segments created in Step 3 and builds out a map of the processes that uniquely fit into each specific segment.

With the logic flow defined in Step 3, every product or customer needs to be run through the flowchart of Step 5. This process flow will allocate each product, customer, or supplier to a specific segment (Step 7). Then the segmentation structure needs to be tested and validated to make sure that the segmentation groupings make sense. For example, if you only have a few products or customers in one of the segments, or if one segment has the vast majority of the products or customers, then a reevaluation of the segmentation structure and the segmentation logic flow may be needed.

Having confirmed that we have a valid segmentation structure in the Build process, and having allocated all the products, customers, or suppliers to their appropriate segments, we are now ready to put the segmentation structure into Execute mode (Steps 8 to 11). This will be discussed in detail in Chapter 7. We start the Execute process first by analyzing the data in a "production" environment and running it through the map to validate its consistency (Step 8). Step 9 is where we analyze the performance results. This is important because if the SCS structure we have designed is not accomplishing the goals that we set out to achieve in Step 1, then we need to go back to the drawing board and investigate what we may have done incorrectly. Step 10 is the feedback mechanism that accomplishes this goal. In reality, today's SCS structure, no matter how well designed, will need to be redesigned and restructured constantly as our product mix or customer base changes. This leaves us with Step 11, which is the final validation of the success or failure of the SCS model.

Cleanse and Analyze Data

As mentioned, the final step in the SCS Analyze process is focused on the data. Data cleansing is primarily an analytics function and it is critically important. In my experience, there are numerous areas in the data that require validation. For example:

- Missing Data
  - Elements of the Master Data are often missing. For example, I often find that lead-time information does not distinguish between production lead time and logistics lead time (or many other elements of lead time). Often these numbers are just plugged in to satisfy the needs of an ERP system and have nothing to do with reality. This can make delivery scheduling difficult.
  - Customer or parts classifications can be inaccurate causing them to be segmented into inappropriate groupings.
- Data Accuracy
  - There is a tendency to be sloppy about data collection in areas that have traditionally added very little value in the measurement process. For example, order data values may be overrated or obscured by not recording a complete set of transactions. Often cancelled ordered data or order postponement data are not recorded. Additionally, sales events like promotions or conferences distort order history by overstating the normal sales activity.

- If the data is distorted, then it will report unnecessarily high data variability, which directly influences forecasts and safety stock calculations and can make them meaningless.
- Data Completeness
  - Often portions of the data are not complete. For example, incomplete information about a customer may cause the customer to be thrown into the wrong tier thereby causing the customer to receive a lower level of customer service than intended.

The process of data cleansing requires several stages of analysis. For example:

1. Identify all the data elements that will be needed for the accurate segmentation of the product, customer, or supplier (from Step 2 and 3 of Chart 5.33).
2. Validate that those data elements exist in our Master Data.
3. Review the calculation process of each data element. Identify what is included in the calculation and identify what may be missing.
4. Analyze the data graphically and use various statistical/analytics tools to identify anomalies in the data.
5. Develop a methodology for reducing or eliminating the errors in the data.
6. Execute the data cleansing process.
7. Review the cleansed data by going back through Step 4 of this process.
8. Repeat Steps 4 to 7 until you have a valid set of data that can be used for the SCS exercise.

Summary

Looking back at Chart 5.34, we have now worked our way through the Analyze phase of SCS. In this phase, we tried to:

- Identify and confirm the goals of the SCS exercise.
- Define the Segmentation Attributes.

- Use Return on Availability to create an SCS model.
- Build out an SCS matrix.
- Segment the SCS matrix into logical segmentation groupings.
- Cleanse the data, making sure that the necessary data elements exist, which would allow the SCS process to move forward and provide us with a meaningful segmentation structure.

At this point, we are ready to move forward to the Build phase of the SCS structure that we will later execute. I hope that this will achieve the goals and objectives behind doing segmentation in the first place.

By three methods we may learn wisdom: First, by reflection, which is noblest; second, by imitation, which is easiest; and third by experience, which is the bitterest.

Confucius

6

An Applied Example of SCS

The Build Process

The wicked leader is he who the people despise.
The good leader is he who the people revere.
The great leader is he who the people say, "We did it ourselves."

Lao Tsu

I hope that you do not feel that you have completed your SCS journey. Referring to Chart 6.1 we see that we have not achieved the goal of defining our segmented structure. In reality, the work is just beginning. As we move into the Build phase of SCS (see Chart 6.2), the analytics teams and the business teams become the best of friends. They end up spending a lot of time together, testing theories and principles that they hope will facilitate their construction of a successful SCS methodology. As shown in Chart 6.2, the SCS approach has three steps in the Build plan. The first of these is to build a segmentation map (Step 5) based on the SCS matrix that was generated in Step 3. Using that map, we define and map out the planning and scheduling strategies that will be executed for each segment (Step 6). In the last step in the Build process, we build, run, test, and validate that the SCS structure we have developed is working in the desired way. Otherwise, we need to return to Step 5, or possibly even back to Step 3 to rethink those elements that are not working correctly.

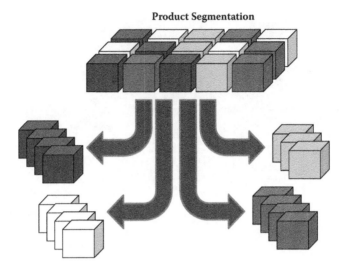

Chart 6.1 Product Segmentation

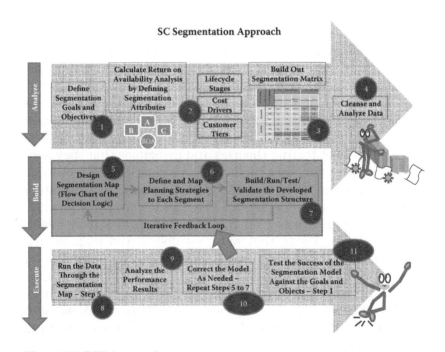

Chart 6.2 SCS Approach

Example — Service level Segmentation, rationalized and simplified into 6 unique segments

Lifecycle Stage	Cost of Availability	Tier 1 Customers			Tier 2 Customers			Tier 3 Customers		
		Availability	Lead Time	SC Business Model	Availability	Lead Time	SC Business Model	Availability	Lead Time	SC Business Model
Launch	Low	High	5 Days	1 Custom	Medium	25 Days	4 Agile			
	Med									
	High									
Active	Low	High	25 Days	Efficient 2						
	Med									
	High				Medium	30 Days	5 Efficient			
End of Life	Low							Low	40 Days	6 Efficient
	Med	High	35 Days	3 Agile						
	High									

Chart 6.3 SCS Example Broken into Segments

Chart 6.3, which is a redrawing of Chart 5.18, shows the output of Step 3 of Chart 6.2. In this chart, we see the segmentation structure that we came up with and we see the Supply Chain characteristics that were derived for each segment. This chart becomes the foundation of the work we need to do in both Steps 5 and 6 of Chart 6.2.

Designing the Segmentation Logic Map

The Segmentation Map is a flow chart of the decision and logic that goes behind SCS. In the example that we were working through in Chapter 5, which resulted in Chart 6.3, we were building a segmentation structure. At this point, we need to think through and build this logic map. Chart 6.4 shows the logic chart for the example of Chart 6.3. Following this logic chart, the parts that are analyzed should end up in the proper segments. You should go through the chart and see how the logic flows. Then, once this logic flow has been built, it becomes necessary to turn this into a piece of software. In order to

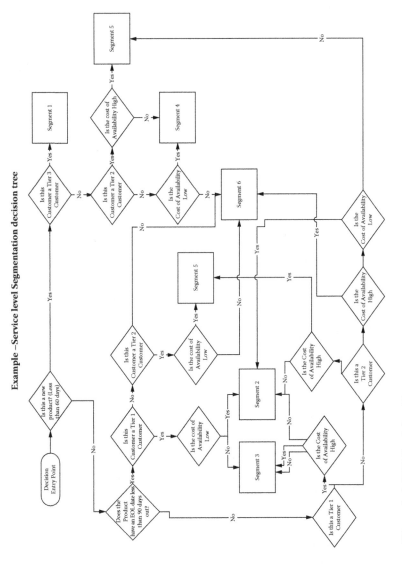

Chart 6.4 SCS Decision Tree

accomplish that, we need to define what pieces of data are needed. In the example of Chart 6.4, we see data elements needed for each of the decision points, such as:

- Product release date for NPI definition
- Product EOL date for EOL definition
- Customer tier
- Return on Availability

There may be situations where these parameters do not easily fit into your database. For example, if a product is not customer specific then customer tiers will be challenging to identify. In cases like that, we may want to use decision fields like product stability or variability. Instead of having customer tiers as one of our dimensions, perhaps we may want to use categories such as:

- Stable product (low variability)
- Medium variability
- High or sporadic variability or variability unknown

At this point, our segmentation structuring is defined. Next, we take the entire cleansed parts database (Step 4 of Chart 6.2) and run each SKU through the SCS logic map (Step 5 of Chart 6.2 as shown in Chart 6.4). At this point, we would have classified each of the SKUs and we are ready to test our production processes on each of them. However, before we do that, let us revisit our case examples and see what each of their maps looks like.

We start by pulling in each of the respective segmentation matrices. For our aerospace example, we pull in Chart 5.25 and redisplay it as Chart 6.5. The corresponding logic flow chart is shown as Chart 6.6. Again, I want to emphasize that this is a simplistic version of what actually happened when we applied SCS at this customer site. For instance, they had many more than three supplier tiers. They evaluated supplies based on reliability, on-time delivery, product quality, and the criticality of the components that they were supplying. They ended up with a matrix of supplier tiers. Each element in the matrix had to be evaluated as to their Supply Chain characteristics.

Example – Segmentation Matrix to
maximize return on availability – Aerospace

Lifecycle Stage	Cost of Availability	Tier 1 Suppliers			Tier 2 Suppliers			Tier 3 Suppliers		
		Criticality	Lead Time	SC Business Model	Criticality	Lead Time	SC Business Model	Criticality	Lead Time	SC Business Model
Launch	Low	High	120 Days	Custom	Medium	120 Days	Efficient	Medium	120 Days	Efficient
	Med	High	120 Days	Custom	Medium	120 Days	Efficient	Low	120 Days	Efficient
	High	High	120 Days	Custom	Medium	120 Days	Efficient	Low	120 Days	Efficient
Active	Low	High	10 Days	Efficient	High	20 Days	Efficient	Low	30 Days	Efficient
	Med	High	10 Days	Agile	High	20 Days	Efficient	Medium	30 Days	Efficient
	High	High	10 Days	Agile	Medium	20 Days	Agile	Low	30 Days	Efficient
End of Life	Low	High	20 Days	Efficient	Low	30 Days	Efficient	Low	40 Days	Efficient
	Med	High	30 Days	Efficient	Low	40 Days	Efficient	Low	45 Days	Efficient
	High	High	40 Days	Efficient	Low	50 Days	Efficient	Low	50 Days	Efficient

Chart 6.5 Aerospace Broken into Segments

Another difference between this case example and the actual work we did at the customer site was that in the actual executed example there were more than three Supply Chain characteristics. There were characteristics related to international scheduling, reliability of the logistics network, border crossing difficulties, etc. There were also characteristics related to demand variability. All of these needed to be evaluated and considered as we built out each of the segments.

Going on to our second example, we look at Chart 5.29, reprinted as Chart 6.7. In this case, we were evaluating the logistics issues for a pharmaceutical organization. The logic flow diagram for this example is seen in Chart 6.8. In this case, reality was also very simplistic. The analysis process was not that complex. They had three tiers of customers and only a few classifications of products based on criticality to the customer. The example shown here was reasonably close to the reality that we came up with in the actual segmentation exercise.

The third and last example was for the high-tech manufacturer. We see the Segmentation Matrix in Chart 5.32, reprinted as Chart 6.9, and the corresponding Segmentation

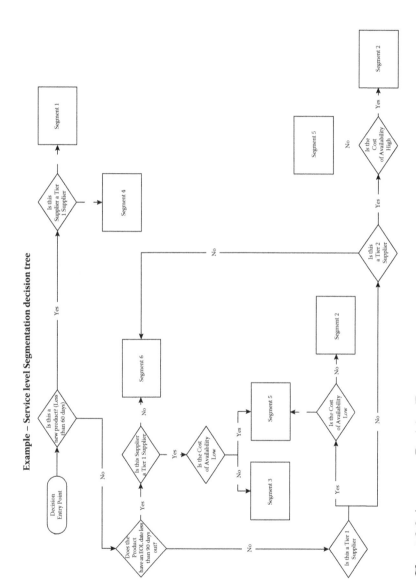

Chart 6.6 Aerospace Decision Tree

Example – Segmentation Matrix to
maximize return on availability – Pharmaceutical

Lifecycle Stage	Cost of Availability	Tier 1 Customer			Tier 2 Customer			Tier 3 Customer		
		Shipping Criticality	Lead Time	SC Business Model	Shipping Criticality	Lead Time	SC Business Model	Shipping Criticality	Lead Time	SC Business Model
Launch	Low	Low	2 Days	Custom	Low	2 Days	Efficient	Low	3 Days	Efficient
	Med	Medium	2 Days	Custom	Medium	2 Days	Efficient	Medium	3 Days	Efficient
	High	High	1 Day	Custom	High	1 Day	Efficient	High	1 Day	Efficient
Active	Low	Low	2 Days	Efficient	Low	2 Days	Efficient	Low	3 Days	Efficient
	Med	Medium	2 Days	Efficient	Medium	2 Days	Efficient	Medium	3 Days	Efficient
	High	High	1 Day	Efficient	High	1 Day	Efficient	High	1 Day	Efficient
End of Life	Low	Low	2 Days	Efficient	Low	2 Days	Efficient	Low	3 Days	Efficient
	Med	Medium	2 Days	Efficient	Medium	2 Days	Efficient	Medium	3 Days	Efficient
	High	High	1 Day	Efficient	High	1 Day	Efficient	High	1 Day	Efficient

Chart 6.7 Pharmaceutical Broken into Segments

Logic Flow diagram in Chart 6.10. This is another case where the matrix is oversimplified in order to keep the example worthy of discussion. In the real case, we did not use customer tiers. Rather, we used product order variability. A highly variable product was segmented differently than one that had a stable and consistent forecast.

Another difference was in the Supply Chain characteristics. In addition to the ones mentioned in Chart 6.9, we also included items like Desired Service Level and Logistics considerations. The matrix in this example became quite complex but we were still able to reduce this complexity to six segments.

Define and Map Planning and Scheduling Strategies for Each Segment

We are now ready to define the Supply Chain planning strategies for each of our SKUs. This is Step 6 of Chart 6.2. This

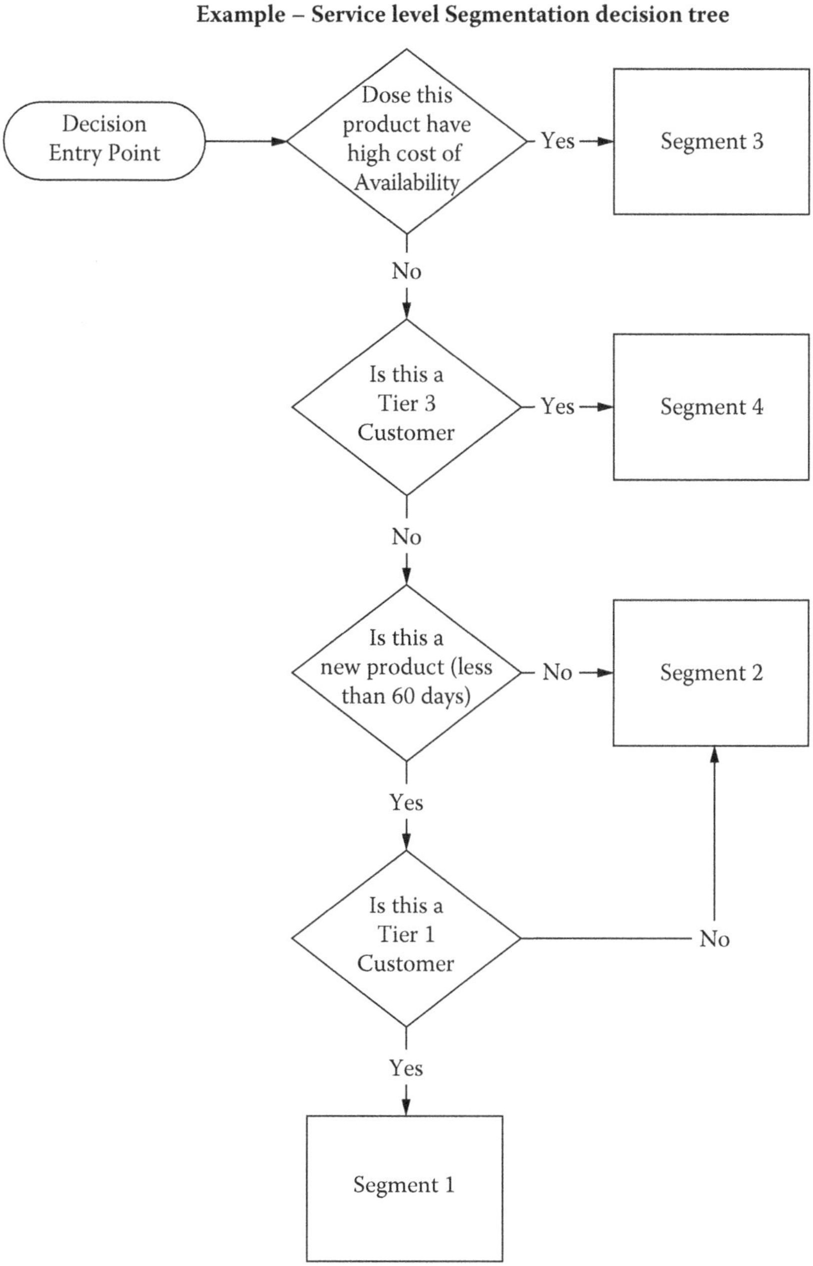

Example – Service level Segmentation decision tree

Chart 6.8 Pharmaceutical Decision Tree

Example – Segmentation Matrix to
maximize return on availability – High Tech

Lifecycle Stage	Cost of Availability	Tier 1 Customer			Tier 2 Customer			Tier 3 Customer		
		Product Availability	Safety Stock/ Inventory Buffering Levels	SC Business Model	Product Availability	Safety Stock/ Inventory Buffering Levels	SC Business Model	Product Availability	Safety Stock/ Inventory Buffering Levels	SC Business Model
Launch	Low	High	Max	Custom	High	Max	Custom	High	Medium	Custom
Launch	Med	High	Max	Custom	High	Max	Custom	High	Medium	Custom
Launch	High	High	Max	Custom	High	Max	Custom	High	Medium	Custom
Active	Low	High	Medium	Agile	High	Medium	Agile	High	Medium	Agile
Active	Med	High	Medium	Agile	High	Medium	Agile	High	Medium	Agile
Active	High	High	Medium	Agile	High	Medium	Agile	High	Medium	Agile
End of Life	Low	Low	Minimum	Efficient	Low	Minimum	Efficient	Low	Minimum	Efficient
End of Life	Med	Low	Minimum	Efficient	Low	Minimum	Efficient	Low	Minimum	Efficient
End of Life	High	Low	Minimum	Efficient	Low	Minimum	Efficient	Low	Minimum	Efficient

Chart 6.9 High-Tech Broken into Segments

Example – Service level Segmentation decision tree

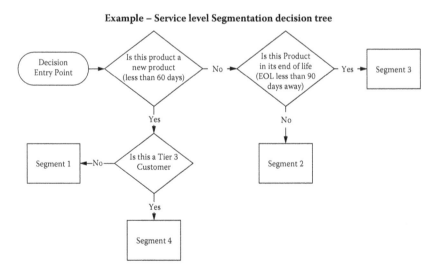

Chart 6.10 High-Tech Decision Tree

step focuses on creating a characteristics map for each of the segments. This map will give us the critical information about the planning structure that will be utilized for each specific segment. For example, we may need to build out characteristics for areas such as the following (this list is not intended to be all-inclusive; it lists areas I have recently encountered but each time I do segmentation something new appears):

Forecasting Options:
    Sales and Operations Planning (S&OP)
    Time Series Options
        Exponential Smoothing
        Multi-period Moving Average
        Regression
    Associative Options
        Econometrics
Production Planning and Scheduling Tool Options:
    Sales and Operations Planning (S&OP)
    Finite Capacity Scheduling (FCS)
    Available to Promise Scheduling (ATP)
    Capable to Promise Scheduling (CTP)
    Material Requirements Planning (MRP)
    Theory of Constraints (TOC)
    Demand Pull Based Environment
    Economic Order Quantity (EOQ)
    Build (Make) To Stock (BTS/MTS) vs Build (Make) to
        Order (BTO/MTO)
    Min/Max
    Optimal Inventory Level (OIL)
    2-Bin
    Reorder Point (ROP)
Operational Process Options
    Vendor Managed Inventories (VMI)
    Lean/Six Sigma Based (LSS)
    Just in Time/Kanban Deliveries (JIT)
    Safety Stock (SS)
Automation Levels
    Manual Data Collection

Shop Floor Data Collection
Manufacturing Execution Systems (MES)
Metrics
　　Motivation-Based Metrics
　　Cycle Time
　　Inventory Levels/Turns
　　Operating Costs
　　Customer Performance Metrics
　　　　Percentage of On-Time Deliveries
　　　　Customer Satisfaction Levels
　　Quality
Number of Touch Points

Not all of these characteristics are relevant for our analysis. Perhaps most of them will not be considered. However, it is important to create a segment characteristics chart so that it can be used to customize and define the characteristics that will become part of the planning and execution structure for each segment. Using our specific, customized characteristics list, we can map out how each of these will fit into our segment structure. An example of this mapping process can be seen in Chart 6.11.

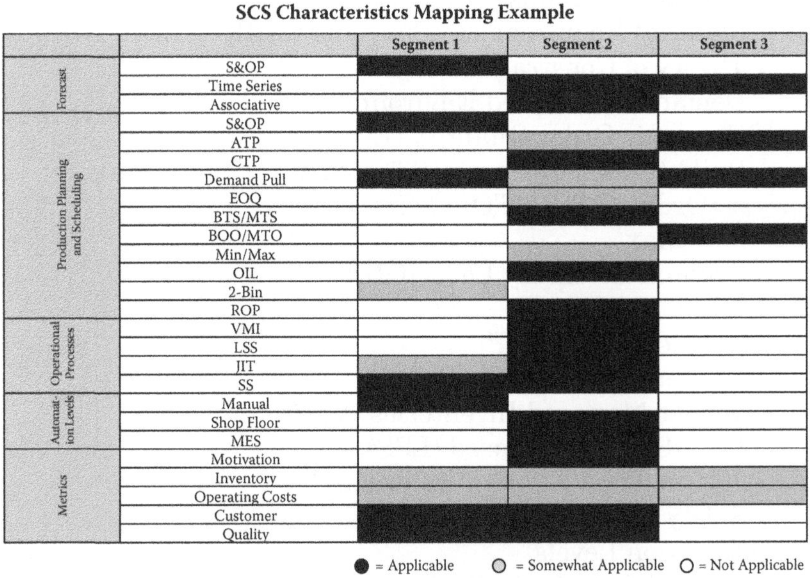

SCS Characteristics Mapping Example

			Segment 1	Segment 2	Segment 3
Forecast		S&OP			
		Time Series			
		Associative			
Production Planning and Scheduling		S&OP			
		ATP			
		CTP			
		Demand Pull			
		EOQ			
		BTS/MTS			
		BOO/MTO			
		Min/Max			
		OIL			
		2-Bin			
		ROP			
Operational Processes		VMI			
		LSS			
		JIT			
		SS			
Automat-ion Levels		Manual			
		Shop Floor			
		MES			
Metrics		Motivation			
		Inventory			
		Operating Costs			
		Customer			
		Quality			

● = Applicable　　◐ = Somewhat Applicable　　○ = Not Applicable

Chart 6.11 SCS Characteristics Mapping

With the characteristics map established for each segment, we can start to see how each of the segments will be managed differently. This also may turn out to be an iterative process. We may not immediately determine what the best planning and scheduling tools are for each segment. This is another area where analytics becomes important. For example, we should take the last year's worth of data and run it against the model as if it were completely new data. We can see if the new segment would perform better using the planning structure of Chart 6.11, or if another planning structure would be more appropriate. We should also benchmark the new approach against the results that you were achieving previously. If you are not doing better, then why change?

Additionally, as part of this exercise, we need to map out a strategy or goal set for each of the segments. For example, in Chart 6.12 we can see what the goal mapping may look like for our example. This goal mapping will be important later (Chart 6.2, Steps 9 and 11) to see if our product or customer distribution into segments comes out as desired or if there will need to be an adjustment in the defined criteria (Chart 6.2, Step 10).

At this point, it would be valuable to create a table that highlights the various options listed in Charts 6.11 and 6.12 including a brief definition, some operational characteristics, and some associated metrics. With these definitions, you will be better able to decide what belongs on your version of Charts 6.11 and 6.12. This table is not intended to be all-inclusive and a further study of the definitions and uses of each item may be valuable. However, this table will at least offer a starting point for a more in-depth discussion and consideration of each of these Supply Chain characteristics.

SCS Goal Mapping Example

		Segment 1	Segment 2	Segment 3
	Planning Cadence	Bi-Weekly	Weekly	On Demand
	% of SKUs	15%	60%	25%
Targets	% of Revenue	40%	50%	10%
	% of Inventory	30%	60%	10%
	% of Planning Effort	50%	20%	30%
	Touch Level of Planners	High	Low	Medium

Chart 6.12 SCS Goal Mapping Example

SCM Operational Tool		Definition	Operational Characteristics
Forecast	S&OP	S&OP is a collaborative forecasting and planning tool where production estimates and schedules are set based on group brainstorming exercises. Sales and Operations work together to come up with these schedules.	This model requires a high degree of manual intervention. It is used when automated methods like OIL and Min/Max do not have a sufficient amount of data to calculate estimated order sizes. It is primarily used for new products on non-repetitive niche products.
	Time Series	Time Series is a forecasting tool that projects the future based on past activities. It uses history to make a prediction about the future assuming that the future will continue similar to the past.	For Time Series to perform well, we need at least two years' (and preferably more) activity. Otherwise, seasonality cannot be built into the model and predictions will be based strictly on averages.
	Exponential Smoothing (ES)	Exponential Smoothing makes forecasting predictions based on the most recent activity and the most recent predictions. In spite of its simplicity, it often does a better job of predicting the future than the more sophisticated modeling techniques.	ES is one of the most simplistic tools to use because it only uses last month's activity and forecast to predict the future using a weighting system that gives more weight to activity that is more recent than older activity. It should always be included as one of the forecasting model options.
	Multi-period Moving Average	Moving Average is a technique that averages recent history in order to make a prediction about the future. Multi-period means that you can use any number of periods (2 or more) to make the predictions.	Multi-period Moving Average can be used either as an averaging tool where you average the last few periods to predict the future, or it can be weighted where the most recent period is weighted more heavily than the periods further back.

Regression	Regression is a forecasting tool that looks at the entire collection of data and attempts to draw a line through that data. Then, projecting that line out into the future would give you your forecast.	Simple Linear Regression is by far the most common form of regression and the line that is generated is a straight line. It is important to take seasonality out of the data before making this projection or the slope of the line will be distorted.
Associative (Econometrics)	Associative forecasting is where, rather than looking at the past to make your prediction, you look at events and trends that are going on around you to make the prediction. For example, the number of housing starts would predict the amount of lumber that would be consumed.	In associative forecasting, you look for any number of variables that may have predictive value. Then you test the validity of that variable using multiple regression and if the variable has predictive value, then you include it in your model when you make your forecast projection.
Production Planning and Scheduling	S&OP	As mentioned earlier, S&OP is a collaborative tool for forecasting. This is also true when it comes to Production Planning and Scheduling. Once again, the sales and operations teams are brought together to build the production plan.	S&OP consumes a lot of time and is a very "hands on" approach. It is filled with personal opinions and therefore is not as scientific and data-based as the other methods we will be discussing. For these reasons, it should be avoided if possible.

Continued

SCM Operational Tool		Definition	Operational Characteristics
Production Planning and Scheduling (*Continued*)	FCS	FCS is a leading-edge tool that eliminates the fallacy of infinite capacity, which is commonly found in other planning and scheduling tools like MRP. FCS builds in real capacity values and adjusts production plans based on actual rather than on estimated values.	FCS requires more data than the other methods. It requires actual movement of materials (event management tracking) and it requires actual capacity information including information about capacity disruptions. However, the reward is an accurate and executable schedule.
	ATP	ATP is a tool where upstream schedules and customer deliveries are based on downstream (supplier) actual inventory availability. Suppliers transmit inventory information to the upstream manufacturer allowing the manufacturer increased accuracy in its planning and scheduling.	ATP requires a sophisticated level of data integration throughout the Supply Chain. The manufacturer needs to know the accurate inventory levels of all the suppliers. This information is utilized to accurately plan and schedule customer deliveries.
	CTP	CTP is a step up from ATP. In CTP, we look at supplier capacity rather than looking at supplier inventory. We use supplier capacity information to determine if the supplier is "capable" of delivering the products we need. Then, based on that supply information we determine our production schedules.	In CTP, we need sophisticated suppliers that have detailed tracking information about their productive capacity. An MES system is a basic requirement if we are to see what capacity is available and what commitments have already been made to utilize that capacity. We also need internal capability to be able to manage and analyze supplier CTP information.

MRP	MRP is the planning and scheduling tool that is considered fundamental to most ERP systems. It is the traditional tool used in the US and Europe for this function and is based on product (materials) definitions.	MRP looks strictly at materials management and assumes infinite capacity in its planning and scheduling process. This can be a major downfall. It is designed to optimize labor production and schedule materials to keep the workforce busy.
TOC	TOC is a planning and scheduling tool developed in Israel and focused on the assumption that the bottleneck is the most critical element in the factory, and that all production and scheduling should be driven to optimize the throughput of the bottleneck.	TOC is an optimization modeling tool and a philosophy. The philosophy says that we must do whatever we can to make sure the bottleneck is as productive as possible. Everything else in the plant exists solely to make the bottleneck effective.
Demand Pull	Demand Pull, often referred to as JIT (Just in Time) or Kanban production, is a system developed in Japan with a focus on materials efficiency. Unlike MRP, which is focused on labor efficiency, Demand Pull looks to keep inventory at a minimum even if it means that labor is occasionally nonproductive.	Demand Pull is utilized when materials are the critical resource in the factory. This means that materials would be the highest value added resource component of the produced item. In that case, we optimize the flow of materials by using Kanbans, which limit the amount of inventory on the floor. Materials are minimized at the expense of less costly resources.

Continued

SCM Operational Tool		Definition	Operational Characteristics
Production Planning and Scheduling (*Continued*)	EOQ	EOQ is one of the oldest inventory planning and scheduling tools and was the basic tool for production prior to the advent of the computer, which allowed calculations that are more elaborate. It is still the foundation of many of the calculations used in tools like MRP and JIT.	EOQ is focused on inventory minimization. It calculates the inventory level that would give us the low-cost batch size for inventory ordering, whether it is a purchase order or a production order. The objective of EOQ is to minimize the total cost of inventory.
	BTS/MTS	BTS and MTS are where the finished good product is manufactured and stored in advance to cover for an anticipated demand. In this model, the optimum level of units is based on the EOQ model and determines how much finished goods inventory is to be stocked.	BTS and MTS are primarily used during the growth or stability phases of a product when we are reasonably sure that the product will be sold within a reasonable period and not give us any obsolescence. BTS is only used when there is a minimal risk in the sales/ordering process.
	BTO/MTO	BTO and MTO are where the products are built only to fill an order from the customers. Nothing is produced without a customer order. This generally means that the lead-time is longer because production time is also part of the lead-time.	BTO and MTO products are generally in decline or in the EOL phase of their product lifecycle. Demand tends to be highly volatile and intermittent. Margins are minimal. Often these are replacement parts and the cost of the part is higher or equal to the revenue.

Min/Max	For Min/Max, the inventory stocking levels are maintained within a range to minimize obsolescence. These are products that are in decline and so Min/Max offers a conservative level of precaution.	Min/Max protects a declining product from excessive obsolete inventory. However, the risk of stock out is greater than with other planning methods such as OIL or MRP.
OIL	OIL is an EOQ-based planning methodology used for stable, low variability products. It minimizes stock outs while at the same time minimizing safety stock and therefore inventory costs. Planning is often automated.	OIL applies to mature, non-seasonal products. Because of a high level of automation, the touch time for planners is minimal. It would be ideal to drive as many products into this segment as possible.
2-Bin	The 2-Bin system is a simplistic system used for inexpensive, high volume, commodity parts like screws. You have two bins of the parts. When the first bin empties out, you start using the second bin and place an order for another bin of parts at the same time.	The 2-Bin system is simplistic and has minimal touch time for the planners. The order trigger is the opening of the second bin. However, since safety stock is immediately set by bin size (which is often the minimum order size), you only use this for extremely inexpensive parts.
ROP	ROP is an EOQ-based system that is another variant of EOQ, and similar to OIL. In ROP, we are working with low variability parts and the trigger point for reordering is set by inventory level, which is a product of lead-time.	ROP calculates the reorder point based on back scheduling the lead-time and determining the average usage over that lead-time. The inventory level of that average usage becomes the reorder point. This assumes a stable usage and attempts to minimize on-hand inventory.

Continued

SCM Operational Tool		Definition	Operational Characteristics
Operational Processes	VMI	VMI is where the raw materials inventory that is within the walls of your facility is actually managed by the vendor supplying those materials.	With VMI, we are generally focused on a Demand Pull environment using Kanbans to pull the materials out of the vendor's on-site inventory.
	LSS	Lean and Six Sigma processes are utilized to eliminate waste and increase the value added content of your processes. It is a change management methodology.	Lean is focused on process optimization through cycle time compression. Six Sigma is focused on variability reduction using statistical methods. Both tools focus on reducing waste and increasing quality.
	JIT /Kanban	As mentioned earlier, JIT and Kanban are the tools of a Demand Pull environment, which is focused on inventory optimization.	JIT also has its roots in EOQ and uses EOQ calculations to define the optimal Kanban size. JIT also focuses on balancing production flow.
	SS	SS is a buffer inventory that is utilized to protect against stock-outs. SS can be a component of any of the other tools, like OIL, Min/Max, MRP, etc. SS is often abused because it is a protective buffer, but it can be extremely expensive in inventory costs.	SS calculations are dependent on the service level that we want to attain, which is specific to the tier level of the customer. It is also dependent on the utilization variability of the product.

Automation Levels	Manual Data Collection	This is where we are using handwritten recordings of productive activities, like inventory movement and job stops or starts.	There is an obvious delay in taking hand-recorded information and inputting it into the database. This time delay is often unacceptable if we are trying to maintain tight control of our production processes.
	Shop Floor Data Collection	In this case, we are using automated data collection equipment and storing that information into a batch database to be analyzed at some future point.	This method is a dramatic improvement over the manual system, but it is still limiting in that it does not offer immediate operational feedback.
	MES	MES is shop floor data collection with immediately available information and reporting including alerts in the event of problems.	MES allows the manufacturer tight control of all the events on the production floor. MES is critical if you are planning to use CTP and give productive feedback including capacity utilization information to the customer.
Metrics	Motivation-Based Metrics	The metrics used in most organizations were developed ad hoc by an accounting or cost control department without any consideration for the effect it would have on the workers. Metrics are motivators and the wrong metrics will motivate the wrong response.	Accounting-based metrics must be eliminated. Employees use metrics as their guide for performance. If it is measured, it must be important. This can be used to advantage. By selecting the correct metrics, organizational transformations can be triggered.
	Cycle Time	Process cycle time is a standard metric that fits most performance measurement guidelines.	Cycle time is the key metric used to measure Lean process improvements.

Continued

SCM Operational Tool

		Definition	Operational Characteristics
Metrics (*Continued*)	Inventory Levels/Turns	Inventory is often the largest cost component in most productions. Therefore, keeping inventory costs under control is critical. A measure of inventory levels assists in controlling this cost.	Inventory turns show the turnaround of inventory. The goal of every organization should be to increase the turns ratio by becoming efficient in inventory movement. This directly measures inventory level.
	Operating Costs	The cost of operations is another key performance metric. Cost of operations needs to focus on the organization's critical resources and does not need all the detail that activity-based costing provides.	For most organizations, the critical resources are materials, labor, and machinery. For other organizations, energy or logistics may be critical as well. Criticality is determined by the value added content each resource contributes to the total product cost.
	Customer Performance Metrics	Ultimately, customer satisfaction is the key performance metric of any Supply Chain.	Motivation metrics, as discussed earlier, should always contain some element of customer satisfaction.
	* Percentage of On-Time Deliveries	On time delivery of the correct product with no quality errors is the ultimate measure of customer satisfaction and the key metric for defining a successful Supply Chain.	Often this number is corrupted because there are many reschedules and recommits. The true number should be "percentage of on-time deliveries to the originally requested delivery date."

* Customer Satisfaction Levels	Customer satisfaction measures are usually achieved by using some type of survey tool.	Surveys do not always offer a complete story of customer satisfaction. Customer satisfaction should also be monitored by looking at operations metrics like customer usage declines.
Quality	Quality is one of the key performance metrics. However, quality needs to be measured from the customer's perspective.	Quality can internally be measured based on engineering specs. However, often these specs do not reflect quality from the customer's perspective and we need to get customer opinions involved in our evaluation of quality.
Number of Touch Points	Touch points are a measure of how often the user has to "touch" the system. This could include the number of handwritten items, number of computer interactions, or number of machine adjustments.	Touch points are failure points. Every time something needs to be "touched," it can also be touched incorrectly. Minimization of touch points, such as automated data collection, has a direct effect on performance and output quality.
Targets Planning Cadence	Planning Cadence is how often production plans are generated. Some production scheduling methods are more conducive to long cycle times (like MRP) and some work better for short cycle times (like Demand Pull).	Planning cadence should be specifically related to the cycle time of production. If the cycle time is short, the cadence should be more often than if the cycle time is long.
% of SKUs	How many SKUs do we want in each segment?	This is an excellent application of the 80-20 Rule, also known as the Pareto Principle.

Continued

SCM Operational Tool		Definition	Operational Characteristics
Targets (Continued)	% of Revenue	What should the revenue coverage be for each segment?	This is an excellent application of the 80-20 Rule, also known as the Pareto Principle.
	% of Inventory	What should the inventory coverage be for each segment?	This is an excellent application of the 80-20 Rule, also known as the Pareto Principle.
	% of Planning Effort	How much of our planner's workload should be focused on this product segment?	The amount of planning effort (calculations, computer interactions, follow-up with suppliers or customers, etc.) should be minimized so that the planner can spend most of his or her time on the high margin, new introduction products that will have the most long-term benefit for the organization.
	Touch Level of Planners	How much of our planner's "touch time" should be focused on this product segment?	A goal should be to minimize the planner's work by automating as much of the planning process as possible. Automated rules-based methodologies tend to perform significantly better than human involved methodologies because of their consistency (assuming they are set up correctly).

Now that we have some familiarity with some of the Supply Chain characteristics that may come into play when we do a characteristics mapping for our segments, we can go back and look at our three examples and see how mappings can occur in each of these cases.

Our first case example is the aerospace example. If we reflect back on Chart 6.5 using the segment structure generated in this segmentation matrix, we are able to identify and work out the Supply Chain characteristics for our aerospace example, as shown in Chart 6.13. The corresponding goals for this segmentation structure are shown in Chart 6.14.

SCS Characteristics Mapping Example – Aerospace

Supply Chain Characteristics		Aerospace Segmentation Example – Segment #					
		1	2	3	4	5	6
Forecast	S&OP						
	Time Series						
	Associative						
Production Planning and Scheduling	S&OP						
	ATP						
	CTP						
	Demand Pull						
	EOQ						
	BTS/MTS						
	BOO/MTO						
	Min/Max						
	OIL						
	2-Bin						
	ROP						
Operational Processes	VMI						
	LSS						
	JIT						
	SS						
Automation Levels	Manual						
	Shop Floor						
	MES						
Metrics	Motivation						
	Inventory						
	Operating Costs						
	Customer						
	Quality						

Chart 6.13 Aerospace Characteristics Mapping

SCS Goal Mapping Example -Aerospace

Supply Chain Characteristics		Aerospace Segmentation Example					
		1	2	3	4	5	6
Targets	Planning Cadence	Bi-Weekly	Bi-Weekly	Weekly	Bi-Weekly	Bi-Weekly	On Demand
	% of SKUs	15%	40%	5%	15%	20%	5%
	% of Revenue	20%	50%	3%	10%	15%	2%
	% of Inventory	15%	40%	5%	15%	20%	5%
	% of Planning Effort	50%	5%	10%	20%	5%	10%
	Touch Level of Planners	High	Low	Low	Medium	Low	Low

Chart 6.14 Aerospace Goal Mapping

In Chart 6.13, we see the six segments corresponding to the six segments highlighted in Chart 6.5. Looking down the table, we can see that different Supply Chain tools are used for each of the segments. These tools are selected based on the Supply Chain characteristics that we identified in Chart 6.5 for each of the specific segments.

In Chart 6.14, we see the target distribution for parts based on the segmentation structure. We can see that we anticipate the majority of the planners' efforts to be exerted in Segments 1 and 4, and that we expect automation to be the primary driver for managing Segments 2, 3, 5, and 6. We also see that we expect most of our revenue to come out of Segments 1 and 2, which are our new products and our stable products, respectively. This is also where we would expect to have the majority of our inventory.

Moving on to our pharmaceutical example, we reflect back on Chart 6.7 and see this same segmentation structure reflected in the mapping of SCM characteristics in Chart 6.15. Corresponding goals are shown in Chart 6.16.

Since the primary focus in the pharmaceutical example was on logistics optimization, several of the Supply Chain operational tools do not apply. This example is not as interesting as

SCS Characteristics Mapping Example – Pharmaceutical

Supply Chain Characteristics			Pharmaceutical Segmentation Example			
			1	2	3	4
Forecast		S&OP				
		Time Series				
		Associative				
Production Planning and Scheduling		S&OP				
		ATP	N/A	N/A	N/A	N/A
		CTP	N/A	N/A	N/A	N/A
		Demand Pull				
		EOQ				
		BTS/MTS	N/A	N/A	N/A	N/A
		BOO/MTO				
		Min/Max				
		OIL				
		2-Bin				
		ROP				
Automation Levels	Operational Processes	VMI	N/A	N/A	N/A	N/A
		LSS				
		JIT				
		SS				
		Manual				
		Shop Floor	N/A	N/A	N/A	N/A
		MES	N/A	N/A	N/A	N/A
Metrics		Motivation				
		Inventory				
		Operating Costs				
		Customer				
		Quality				

Chart 6.15 Pharmaceutical Characteristics Mapping

SCS Goal Mapping Example – Pharmaceutical

Supply Chain Characteristics		Pharmaceutical Segmentation Example			
		1	2	3	4
Targets	Planning Cadence	Bi-Weekly	Bi-Weekly	Weekly	Bi-Weekly
	% of SKUs	10%	50%	20%	20%
	% of Revenue	15%	50%	15%	20%
	% of Inventory	20%	40%	20%	20%
	% of Planning Effort	50%	10%	10%	30%
	Touch Level of Planners	High	Low	Low	Medium

Chart 6.16 Pharmaceutical Goal Mapping

the aerospace or high-tech examples from a Supply Chain perspective, but the segmentation cost savings benefits are still very significant.

Moving on to our last example, the high-tech example that was developed in Chart 6.9, we again see an interesting distribution of Supply Chain functionality, as mapped out in Chart 6.17. In this example, it is easy to see how each of the segments requires an entirely different set of Supply Chain tools.

This is a good time to reflect back on why we are doing segmentation. As can be seen in Chart 6.17, it would be inappropriate

SCS Characteristics Mapping Example – High Tech

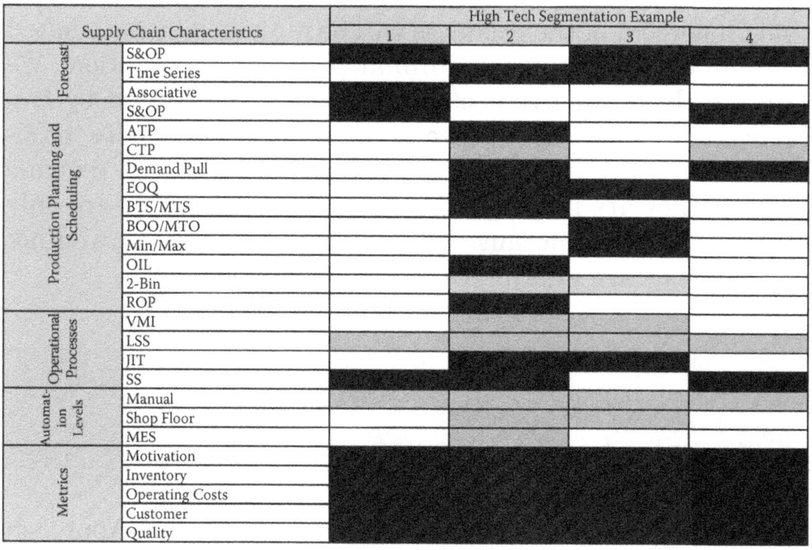

Chart 6.17 High-Tech Characteristics Mapping

SCS Goal Mapping Example – High Tech

Supply Chain Characteristics		High Tech Segmentation Example			
		1	2	3	4
Targets	Planning Cadence	Bi-Weekly	Bi-Weekly	Weekly	Bi Weekly
	% of SKUs	15%	50%	20%	15%
	% of Revenue	25%	60%	5%	10%
	% of Inventory	25%	40%	20%	15%
	% of Planning Effort	50%	10%	15%	25%
	Touch Level of Planners	High	Low	Low	Medium

Chart 6.18 High-Tech Goal Mapping

to apply one generic set of Supply Chain tools to all the products for this high-tech company. Yet, that is what we do. We apply a one-size-fits-all approach to our planning and scheduling, and then we are surprised when it does not work correctly in optimizing all our inventory and customer performance problems.

Chart 6.18 shows that for this high-tech example we are completely refocusing our planning function. We see that 75 percent of the planning function's effort will be focused on 30 percent of the products. In addition, in reverse, we see that 70 percent of the products will be managed by automated techniques that require minimal planner intervention. We also see that 85 percent of the revenue is generated by two segments. Moreover, we see that a disproportionate number of SKUs are in the segment that has nearly no revenue because they are in their EOL stage. These products are only being maintained because of a need for spare parts, and not because they are making the company any money.

Build/Run/Test/Validate the Developed Segmentation Structure

The last step in the Build phase of the Segmentation Approach as shown in Chart 6.2 (reprinted as Chart 6.19) is actually one

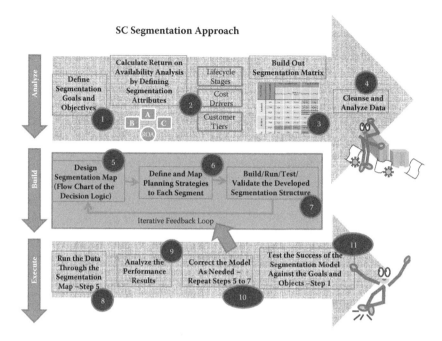

Chart 6.19 SCS Approach

of the most important. It has two parts to it. The first is the running and validation of the segmentation structure that we have developed up to this point. The second is the feedback loop, which modifies and corrects any of the segmentation structure that is not working properly.

This step is heavily entangled with analytics. The approach that has been used for this step includes the following:

1. Download the entire parts inventory into a spreadsheet including all the decision criteria necessary to make segmentation decisions for each part. For Chart 6.4, this would include information about the following:
    a. Is this a new product (less than 60 days)? We need to know what the product introduction date is.
    b. What is the tier level of the customer/supplier that is using this part?
    c. What is the EOL date for this product? Are we within the last 90 days of the product's life?

d. Is the COA Low, Medium, or High for this product? How do we calculate COA? Do we have all the necessary fields associated with each product so that we can make this calculation?

2. Run each product through the logic decision tree in Chart 6.4 to classify each product.

3. Pull in the last 6 to 12 months of order data for each product.

4. Run the production planning structure, as defined in Chart 6.11, and take a close look at the performance of this plan against some key metrics such as:
   a. Inventory level/cost
   b. Number of stock outs
   c. Customer on-time deliveries
   d. Safety stock levels

5. Compare the results from Step 4 (above) with the actual performance of each of the products for the last 6 to 12 months.

6. Analyze the segmentation structure against the goals that were defined for that structure in Chart 6.12.

7. Identify the holes. Are you satisfied with the analysis results identified in Steps 5 and 6 above? If not, why not? Most importantly, how do we fix it? What needs to be changed? Is the logic flow of Chart 6.4 correct? Is our grouping in Chart 6.3 correct? Are the goals in Chart 6.12 reasonable? Everything needs to be questioned and challenged.

8. Fix the problems that were identified in Step 7 above. You see this feedback loop in the bottom of the Build arrow in Chart 6.19. Go back through the segmentation structure and make the appropriate corrections.

9. Do it all again. Rerun Steps 1 through 8 above repeatedly until you have a segmentation structure that performs the way you think it should. This is an iterative process and you will *never* get it right the first time so do not be surprised by the need to revise the model. Press forward and make the appropriate changes. Then run it repeatedly until you get it right.

Summary

Chart 6.19 is a reprint of Chart 6.2. This chapter has been focused on the center box of this diagram—the Build portion. This is an analytics heavy portion of the SCS process. In this portion of the process, we build out the defined segments. We define what each of the segments means and how products are allocated to each of the segments. In addition, we defined how the Supply Chain process works for each of these segments. We identified what the important Supply Chain characteristics are and how they influence SCS. Now we will move on to the Execution portion of SCS, which is where we "go live."

> Plans are only good intentions unless they immediately degenerate into hard work.
>
> **Peter Drucker**

7

SCS Execution

The more I want to get something done, the less I call it work.

Richard Bach

Most of the front-end work in the segmentation process has now been completed. We are close to achieving the structure shown in Chart 7.1. Looking at Chart 7.2 we see that we have developed the Analyze phase and the Build phase. We are now ready to move forward with the Execute phase, which is the topic of this chapter. In the Execute phase, we are executing SCS against our database. The first two phases had us looking backward at history to see how segmentation would perform. In this phase, we are moving forward looking at the day-to-day performance of the segmentation structure. We are applying what we have constructed and validating its performance.

Product Segmentation

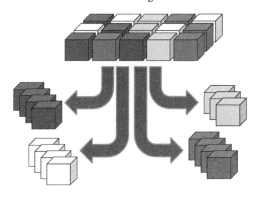

Chart 7.1 Product Segmentation

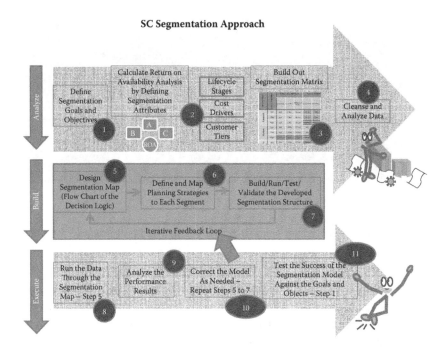

Chart 7.2 SCS Approach

Looking at Chart 7.2, Step 8, we start by running the current data through the segmentation map that was developed in Step 5 (see Chart 7.3, which is a reprint of Chart 6.4). This process should allocate the entire parts database (or customer database or supplier database depending on what we are segmenting) to one of the many segments that we identified in Step 3. This process should be fairly repetitive and routine. We will need to establish a repetitive cycle of how often we need to rerun the segmentation process. Most organizations choose to run it quarterly because they do not want the parts definitions to change any more quickly than that. Moreover, for most organizations where the product lifecycle is in terms of years this would be the best timing.

For organizations that have very short product lifecycles, they may choose to rerun the segmentation allocation step bi-monthly or monthly just to stay on top of the ever-changing product lifecycle changes. For example, as products move from NPI to stability, we want to reduce the planner's influence on the product. Similarly, as we move from declining to EOL

Example – Service level Segmentation decision tree

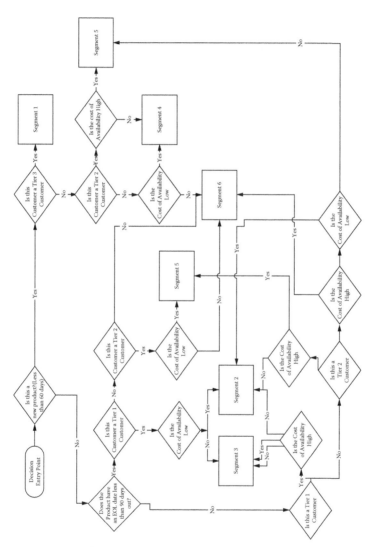

Chart 7.3 SCS Decision Tree

we want to tighten up our inventory control and avoid obsolescence. These are the types of thoughts and considerations that would determine the repetitiveness with which Step 8 in Chart 7.2 is performed.

Moving to Step 9, there are several areas of performance that we want to analyze. The first thing we want to look at is the structural breakdown of our segmented groups. Specifically, we want to review if we satisfied the goals we established for ourselves in Chart 6.12 reprinted as Chart 7.5. Is the SKU count, revenue, inventory dollar distribution reasonably close to what we had targeted? If not, perhaps our distribution of historical data was not a valid sampling of how we need the current data to perform.

The other area of performance analysis that we need to consider in Step 9 is the actual performance of the planning system for each specific segment. Are we achieving the goals that we set for ourselves when we began this segmentation adventure? (These goals were established in Step 1 of Chart 7.2 and need to be confirmed.) For example, are we getting the inventory reductions for each segment that we anticipated based on the Planning Strategy map that we created in Step 6. (See Chart 7.4, which is a reprint of Chart 6.11.) Are we getting the customer service levels that we were shooting for? Have we reduced our number of stock-outs? And so on. On the other hand, are we using the wrong set of planning tools? Each segment's tool set needs to be verified and confirmed.

Step 10 in Chart 7.2 focuses on tweaking the segmentation model to make it just a little bit better. This is not a one-time process. It is an ongoing process with numerous iterations. We should constantly be going back to the performance results and validating that the model is performing as expected. We may even want to experiment and try different mythologies to see if they can perform better than what we are currently running. We cyclically repeat Steps 5 through 7 and then test them out on the data from Steps 8 and 9 until we get to the point where we are satisfied with the results. Again, this is an iterative process and what is optimal today will not be optimal 5 years from now or possibly even 1 year from now.

The last step, Step 11 in Chart 7.2, is another revalidation and confirmation that we have achieved the SCS goals

SCS Characteristics Mapping Example

			Segment 1	Segment 2	Segment 3
Forecast		S&OP			
		Time Series			
		Associative			
Production Planning and Scheduling		S&OP			
		ATP			
		CTP			
		Demand Pull			
		EOQ			
		BTS/MTS			
		BOO/MTO			
		Min/Max			
		OIL			
		2-Bin			
		ROP			
Automation Levels	Operational Processes	VMI			
		LSS			
		JIT			
		SS			
		Manual			
		Shop Floor			
		MES			
Metrics		Motivation			
		Inventory			
		Operating Costs			
		Customer			
		Quality			

● = Applicable   ◐ = Somewhat Applicable   ○ = Not Applicable

Chart 7.4 SCS Characteristics Mapping

SCS Goal Mapping Example

		Segment 1	Segment 2	Segment 3
Targets	Planning Cadence	Bi-Weekly	Weekly	On Demand
	% of SKUs	15%	60%	25%
	% of Revenue	40%	50%	10%
	% of Inventory	30%	60%	10%
	% of Planning Effort	50%	20%	30%
	Touch Level of Planners	High	Low	Medium

Chart 7.5 SCS Global Mapping Example

outlined in Step 1 and the segment-specific goals outlined in Step 6 (as shown in Chart 7.5). In my experience, the expectations and goals that were identified in Step 1 are often over-achieved, and the goals that are identified in Step 6 are often revised. The goals in Step 1 tend to be conservative because the organization is pessimistic about the impact that SCS can achieve. They are often pleasantly surprised.

The goals in Step 6 are often incorrect because the organization learns that it has a poor understanding of its product make-up. Sadly, the organization often discovers that it has a much larger obsolescence issue than it realized. The organization also discovers that it has a large number of SKUs hanging on that should have been taken out of inventory a long time ago. These SKUs have little or no demand but have product sitting in inventory. Storing obsolete inventory because it is painful to throw it away is expensive, both in the loss of inventory carrying cost and in cost of storage space. SCS is often an eye-opening exercise and triggers a cleanup of the inventory system.

In summary, the execution of the SCS system is an analytics exercise of:

1. Allocating the parts to their respective segments
2. Defining the cycle that will be used for rerunning the segmentation exercise
3. Analyzing that the distribution of the parts achieves the desired goals
4. Validating the performance of the segmentation structure against the originally defined SCS goals
5. Validating that the SCS planning and scheduling structure is optimized
6. Tweaking improvements to the SCS structure as needed and rerunning it until you are satisfied with the results
7. Signing off on the SCS structure indicating that you have achieved all the desired goals
8. Revisiting the SCS structure at regular intervals to make sure it is still performing as desired

As the author can testify, if done correctly, SCS can generate enormous improvement results in customer satisfaction, inventory reduction, and on-time customer performance. We next move on to discuss the struggles of applying SCS to your organization.

> If you're trying to achieve, there will be roadblocks. I've had them; everybody has had them. But obstacles don't have to stop you. If you run into a wall, don't turn around and give up. Figure out how to climb it, go through it, or work around it.
>
> **Michael Jordan**

8

SCS in
Your Organization

Leadership is the art of getting someone else to do something you
want done because he wants to do it.

Dwight D. Eisenhower

Chart 8.1 shows that SCS is not just about the backend or
demand side. The frontend or supply side may also require
segmentation, and the two sides of the SCS structure may be
dramatically different.

In this chapter, I am going to present you a scenario that
I have encountered a dozen times. The names have been
changed to protect the innocent. Not all cases are the same.
There is always some level of uniqueness. However, the example
I am presenting here is painfully close to what I have encoun-
tered at numerous companies.

However, before we do that I want to give you something to
work on. This puzzle is a planning/scheduling puzzle that I like
to give my planners to see how good they are. I rarely get the
correct answer. But, just in case you are one of those exceptions,
Chart 8.2 contains the puzzle. The answer comes much later.

Moving on to our case example of SCS, let us assume you are
thinking about trying out segmentation. You are a factory and
have both Demand and Supply side parts. You need to manage
the Demand side to maximize customer satisfaction and optimize on-time delivery. In addition, you want to minimize the
inventory levels on the Supply side. Right now, you are doing
it all using a spreadsheet. You are installing an ERP software

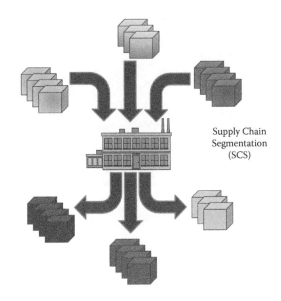

Chart 8.1 SCS Segmentation

The Planner's Nemesis

Arrange the symbols so that you end up with
a row of alternating symbols in four moves,
moving two adjacent symbols in each move.

Chart 8.2 The Planner's Nemesis

environment like SAP or Oracle and you decided that this is a good time to think about SCS. Your ERP contains a planning module, but it has very limited flexibility and offers nothing in the way of segmentation. It claims to have these features, but in reality, it just allows you to place a code into your Master Data for each part that identifies a planning process. It does not tell you which code to place for each part. Moreover, it does not help you identify which planning process should be used for each part. Since you do not want to install a one-size-fits-all planning system that will not manage the various characteristics of your products independently, what do you do?

At this point, you realize that your ERP is not going to give you what you need to accomplish SCS and so you decide that you are going to have to design some kind of bolt-on SCS system. This could take the form of a spreadsheet, some other external software product, or it could be a direct modification to the ERP package. The advantage of the spreadsheet or customized software package is that these are generally more flexible and easier to customize and adapt. The advantage of modifying the ERP package is that no matter which alternative you choose, you will need to pull data from the ERP package, process it through your tool, and then return the segmentation results back to the ERP package. These interfaces are easier by working directly with the ERP package. However, I have found that most companies prefer to go outside of the ERP package because the rules within the ERP environment limit the level of flexibility that segmentation requires.

For an external package, the types of data that will be required from the ERP package include Item Master Data, Customer Master Data, Sales History, etc. The types of data that an external system would return to the ERP system include the Segmentation Code, Safety Stock levels, Service Level information, Planning System, etc.

Analyze

The decision has been made to pursue SCS. Having made that decision you now begin the process of working your way through the flow of Chart 8.3, which is a reprint of Charts 6.2 and 7.2. We start with Step 1, which defines the goals and objectives of executing SCS. This needs to be put into metrics. For example, inventory reduction, logistics cost reductions, on-time delivery improvement, and stock-out reduction are very common metrics that are applied to SCS. Make it measurable by specifying a percentage change to each metric you specify. Do not cloud the message with too many metrics, which may become conflicting. Focus on your specific problem area and the related target improvement.

Step 2 is where we define Return on Availability. This is often a challenging step and in this example, we will make it

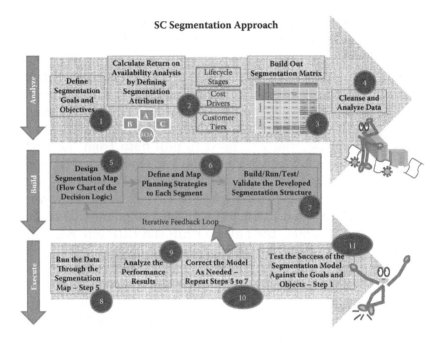

Chart 8.3 SCS Approach

extremely difficult. We will go into a conference room and tell the team that we want to calculate Return on Availability and they all look at us as if we are speaking a foreign language. So, we work our way through the process one step at a time.

In general, by introducing SCS we are introducing a new way of thinking. The creation process is an eye-opening experience for new users. They struggle to think about what they are doing in a new way. It moves them out of the box in which they traditionally see themselves.

We start by looking at Chart 8.4, which is a reprint of Chart 5.7. Earlier when we looked at this chart, we were trying to understand the components of Return on Availability. Similarly, as we try to explain the concept to our imaginary team, we will go through the same exercise.

We start by looking at the first element of our three-pronged approach, which is Item A, managing the product lifecycle stages. Chart 8.5 is an adaptation of Chart 5.8 where we looked at an example of the lifecycle stages. In our group meeting, we ask questions such as:

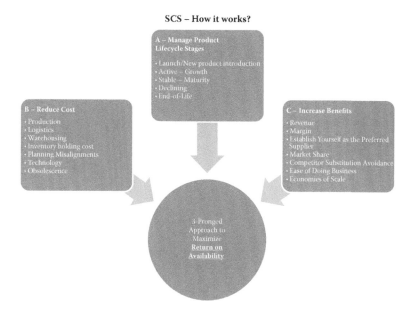

SCS – How it works?

A – Manage Product Lifecycle Stages
- Launch/New product introduction
- Active – Growth
- Stable – Maturity
- Declining
- End-of-Life

B – Reduce Cost
- Production
- Logistics
- Warehousing
- Inventory holding cost
- Planning Misalignments
- Technology
- Obsolescence

C – Increase Benefits
- Revenue
- Margin
- Establish Yourself as the Preferred Supplier
- Market Share
- Competitor Substitution Avoidance
- Ease of Doing Business
- Economies of Scale

3-Pronged Approach to Maximize **Return on Availability**

Chart 8.4 How SCS Works

"What are the significant stages of your product's life?"

"What are the characteristics of the products at each of these stages?"

"Specifically, at what points would you expect the planning approach to change?"

"How should products be managed differently at each of the different stages?"

With the answers to these questions, we can start to build out and define the product lifecycle for your customer. We would end up with something like the table shown in Chart 8.6 (the information from this table is used for Steps 2, 3, and 6 from Chart 8.3).

Having this information sketched out, we now have an understanding of the first dimension on Return on Availability as shown in Chart 8.4. We now move on to the second dimension, which is Reduce Cost. For this analysis, I ask the following questions:

"What are the goals of your segmentation process (Step 1 of Chart 8.3)?"

"Is cost reduction one of those goals?"

"Which costs should we be targeting?"

A – Identify the Lifecycle Stages of the Product

| Introduction NPI Product Phase-In | Growth Accelerating Sales | Maturity High Demand Stable Market | Decline Loosing Market | EOL Product in Phase-Out |

Chart 8.5 Lifecycle Stages

A– Analysis of the Lifecycle Stages of the Product

Lifecycle Stages	Characteristics	Planning Approach
New Product Introduction (NPI)	Less than 3 months on the market, High margins	Heavy sales and operations involvement to make planning decisions because there is no history to work with; S&OP, extremely high touch
Growth	More than 3 months on the market, High margins	Three months worth of history that we can use to predict growth; EOQ or OIL, low touch
Maturity	Demand has leveled out, these products are our cash cows, margin is still strong, low demand variability	Because of the high level of predictability the planning process for these parts should be completely automated; MRP, EOQ, OIL, low touch
Decline	Demand is starting to come down because of competition, either from an internal product or from competitors, margins are coming down, increased variability in product demand	Reducing demand and dropping margins means that we want to be careful not to get stuck with excessive inventories that will eventually become obsolete; Min/Max; BTO/MTO, medium touch
End of Life (EOL)	Little or no demand and what demand there is has become extremely intermittent, margins are approaching zero	We want to stop producing this part and get it off our parts list. We want to burn up whatever inventory we have left and then shut it down; EOL, medium touch

Chart 8.6 Analysis of Lifecycle Stages

Typically, the answer I get is, "Yes, cost is important." When I explore which costs are important, I usually hear the following:

Operating Costs
Materials/Inventory Costs
Logistics Costs

Then I ask questions about the impact of each of these costs on availability to the customer. For example:

"Does the cost of inventory have a high, medium, or low impact (or influence) on the availability of the product to the customer?"
"How does this cost influence our willingness to carry increased or decreased inventories at the effect of customer service?"

For our imaginary example, after our discussion we would end up with something along the lines of Chart 8.7, which is an adaptation of Chart 5.9.

Be careful not to tie yourself down with the belief that you have to come up with a cost driver. I have worked with organizations where cost is not a driver, like government

B – Identify cost drivers that impact return on availability

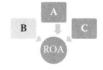

Cost Drivers	Impact of the Driver	Attributes		
Operating Costs	Product availability/obsolesence	Long	Medium	High
Inventory Costs	Level of inventory buffering	Low	Medium	High
Logistics Costs	Interdependencies/stock outs	Low	Medium	High

Cost of Availability			Minimize Cost
High	Medium	Low	

Chart 8.7 Cost Drivers

agencies or large bureaucratic companies that are cash rich, like Saudi Aramco Oil. In these cases, this dimension can be completely dropped.

Next, while I still have everyone in the conference room and before they all start leaving, I start working on the third dimension of the COA calculation (Step 3 in Chart 8.4). This is the benefits side of the equation. The examples we worked on previously have focused on benefits to specific tiers of customers or suppliers. However, in an attempt to do something different in this example, I will assume there is no distinctive grouping of customers. All the customers receive all the products and we do not have specific products that are allocated to specific customers. In this case, we look for other benefits that would satisfy the goals of my SCS exercise. Trying to stay realistic, I worked with one organization that said it wanted to differentiate on a service level. How does the service level link to the lifecycle stage of the product and the cost drivers?

Having built out the three dimensions of Chart 8.4, we are now able to populate the segmentation table (Step 3 of Chart 8.3). At this point, the team is ready for lunch and they have had enough of this "Cost of Availability" stuff. So, I have lunch brought in. I didn't want to let them escape until I had something I could work with. While they are eating lunch, I crank up the computer and project my matrix on the screen. Now we are ready to populate the matrix. The result is shown in Chart 8.8.

Having completed the table, I now release everyone so they can return to their day jobs. I go off to a corner by myself and attempt to make sense of this matrix. I look for ways to break this out into segments. The results of my efforts are shown in Chart 8.9. I proceed to send this segmented matrix out to the team and ask for their approval. They come back with a few tweaks, which I incorporate and send out again. I continue this cycle of correction and improvement until I have everyone in agreement. In the end, we came up with nine segments as shown. Our examples have shown fewer segments, but nine segments are not too many. For this example, it works out well.

Segmentation Matrix

Lifecycle Stage	Cost of Availability	High Service Level			Medium Service Level			Low Service Level		
		Safety Stock	On Time Delivery	SC Business Model	Safety Stock	On Time Delivery	SC Business Model	Safety Stock	On Time Delivery	SC Business Model
NPI	Low	High	99%	Custom	High	97%	Custom	Medium	95%	Custom
NPI	Med	High	99%	Custom	High	97%	Custom	Medium	95%	Custom
NPI	High	High	99%	Custom	High	97%	Custom	Medium	95%	Custom
Growth	Low	High	99%	Agile	Medium	97%	Agile	Medium	95%	Agile
Growth	Med	High	99%	Agile	Medium	97%	Agile	Medium	95%	Agile
Growth	High	High	99%	Agile	Medium	97%	Agile	Medium	95%	Agile
Mature	Low	Low	97%	Agile	Low	97%	Agile	Low	95%	Agile
Mature	Med	Low	97%	Agile	Low	97%	Agile	Low	95%	Agile
Mature	High	Low	97%	Agile	Low	97%	Agile	Low	95%	Agile
Decline	Low	Low	90%	Efficient	Low	80%	Efficient	Low	70%	Efficient
Decline	Med	Low	90%	Efficient	Low	80%	Efficient	Low	70%	Efficient
Decline	High	Low	90%	Efficient	Low	80%	Efficient	Low	70%	Efficient
EOL	Low	Zero	50%	Efficient	Zero	50%	Efficient	Zero	50%	Efficient
EOL	Med	Zero	50%	Efficient	Zero	50%	Efficient	Zero	50%	Efficient
EOL	High	Zero	50%	Efficient	Zero	50%	Efficient	Zero	50%	Efficient

Chart 8.8 Segmentation Matrix

Segmentation Matrix with Segments Broken Out

Lifecycle Stage	Cost of Availability	High Service Level			Medium Service Level			Low Service Level		
		Safety Stock	On Time Delivery	SC Business Model	Safety Stock	On Time Delivery	SC Business Model	Safety Stock	On Time Delivery	SC Business Model
NPI	Low	High	99%	Custom	High	97%	Custom	Medium	95%	Custom
NPI	Med	High 1	99%	Custom	High 2	97%	Custom	Medium 3	95%	Custom
NPI	High	High	99%	Custom	High	97%	Custom	Medium	95%	Custom
Growth	Low	High	99%	Agile	Medium	97%	Agile	Medium	95%	Agile
Growth	Med	High 4	99%	Agile	Medium	97%	Agile	Medium	95%	Agile
Growth	High	High	99%	Agile	Medium	97%	Agile	Medium	95%	Agile
Mature	Low	Low	97%	Agile	Low	97%	Agile	Low 6	95%	Agile
Mature	Med	Low	97%	Agile	Low 5	97%	Agile	Low	95%	Agile
Mature	High	Low	97%	Agile	Low	97%	Agile	Low	95%	Agile
Decline	Low	Low	90%	Efficient	Low	80%	Efficient	Low	70%	Efficient
Decline	Med	Low 7	90%	Efficient	Low	80%	Efficient	Low	70%	Efficient
Decline	High	Low	90%	Efficient	Low 8	80%	Efficient	Low	70%	Efficient
EOL	Low	Zero	50%	Efficient	Zero	50%	Efficient	Zero	50%	Efficient
EOL	Med	Zero	50% 9	Efficient	Zero	50%	Efficient	Zero	50%	Efficient
EOL	High	Zero	50%	Efficient	Zero	50%	Efficient	Zero	50%	Efficient

Chart 8.9 Broken into Segments

We are now ready to move forward to the next step, which is Step 4 in Chart 8.3. As discussed earlier, this is an analytics exercise where we go through the data and look for anomalies that would distort our results. For example, looking at transaction history we should check if sales promotions might cause an abnormal surge in demand. We need to decide if this is a valid part of our business and we want to include this information in our order history, or if this is abnormal and would make our order history excessively high, increasing our forecast projection to a high value that does not represent reality. Another area in transaction data where I have experienced misrepresentations of the data is in identifying which data has been captured. For example, I have found on occasion that we have shipment data, but we do not have order data, which means that we know what was sent out but we do not know what orders were not sent out for whatever reason. So, we do not really know what our total demand was and this can significantly distort our forecast to the point where it is invalid. We want to forecast what we potentially should have shipped, not what we actually shipped which is reduced by the orders we could not fulfill.

Another example of data cleansing is that we take a close look at the Master Data. Often we will find missing elements in the Master Data, which includes missing information like lead times. We may have delivery lead time but we do not have production lead time. Far too often, the lead times are guesses rather than actual. For example, if you look through the Master Data and most of your products have the same lead time, then you can feel confident that the lead time is a plugged number rather than a number that can actually be used for product planning and scheduling.

One thing I can guarantee is that there will be data errors. This goes back to the idea that what isn't actually used is worked around. If the Master Data wants a number, and we do not have a number, we just give it a number so that the problem goes away. Now, when we are trying to introduce SCS we would be searching for data elements that we did not use in the past, and the accuracy of these elements could defuse the accuracy of our planning process. Therefore, a careful review of the data elements is critical.

Build

Now we are ready to move in the Build phase of SCS (Chart 8.3). In Step 5, we work on the segmentation logic flow map. We use the information in Chart 8.9 to create this logic flow. Taking a close look at Chart 8.9, the first thing we notice is that COA is irrelevant. It will not come into play in our logic flow diagram. The logic flow diagram would come out looking something like Chart 8.10.

Using this logic flow, we would need to go back to the Master Data and ask questions like:

- How do we determine (using some form of calculation) if this product is a new product? It is easy to say that we classify a product as a new product if it is less than 60 days old, but do we have the information in our Master Data to tell us that this product is within that time period? What do we need to do to our Master Data to create this level of information? Do we need a product initiation date?
- How do we access EOL information? Is there a date in the product master that specifically tells us the expiration date of the product? What do we use to calculate that we are in the product's last 90 days? Who would be the right person to input that data and to ensure its accuracy?
- What information do we have in the Master Data that tells us the desired service level of a particular product? Do we get that by tying the product to a specific customer? Or do some products lock the customer into a product line causing these to have a higher service level than components? For example, certain types of equipment, like a camera, require add-on equipment like lenses to specifically fit that camera. The camera would have a higher service level than the lenses. But how do we translate this into the Master Data for the product so we can use this information in our logic flow?

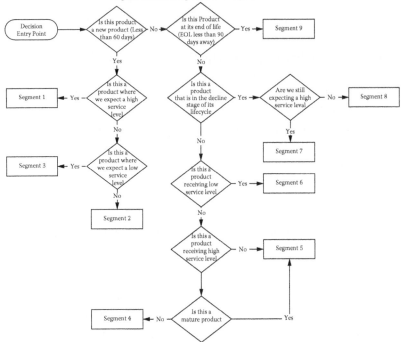

Chart 8.10 Decision Tree

As we go through the process of identifying the necessary data elements, we may need to dig a little deeper in our analysis. For example, the table in Chart 8.11 shows the logic behind identifying the lifecycle stages.

Since this is a fictional example based on a collection of real experiences, the information supplied may be significantly different than what you experience within your organization, but this example should feel real enough for you to start building your own logic flow within your organization. At this point, we should be ready to run our Inventory Master Data File through our segmentation logic and see what the distribution of that master file looks like. However, that does not occur until Step 7 of Chart 8.3 and we need to complete Step 6 first. We need the information from Step 6 to do the validation that needs to be done in Step 7.

Chart 8.12 details the planning systems requirements that we expect for each segment. This will be used as we design the

Lifecycle Logic Analysis

Lifecycle Stage	Analytical Characteristics
NPI	Within the first 60 days of product release as calculated based on the product release date
Growth	Increasing demand for the product, somewhat high variability, and high margins
Mature	Low product usage variability, flat forecast, and fairly high margins
Decline	Declining sales order demand, low margins, and increased usage variability
EOL	Within the last 90 days of the product's life as calculated based on the product termination date

Chart 8.11 Lifecycle Logic

Planning Systems Requirements

	Supply Chain Characteristics	Segmentation Example – Segment #								
		1	2	3	4	5	6	7	8	9
Forecast	S&OP									
	Time Series									
	Associative									
Production Planning and Scheduling	S&OP									
	ATP									
	CTP									
	Demand Pull									
	EOQ									
	BTS/MTS									
	BTO/MTO									
	Min/Max									
	OIL									
	2-Bin									
	ROP									
Operational Processes	VMI									
	LSS									
	JIT									
	SS									
Automation Levels	Manual									
	Shop Floor									
	MES									

Chart 8.12 Planning System Requirements

customized planning and scheduling methodology, which will be executed through the ERP system. ERP systems will take the input from the segmentation analysis and use these values to calculate order sizes, safety stocks, etc.

Chart 8.13 breaks out the goals that we are expecting to achieve through the SCS process for each specific segment. With these goals and the information from Chart 8.10 and Chart 8.11, we are now able to run Step 7 of Chart 8.3. This

Planning Systems SCS Goals

Supply Chain Characteristics		Segmentation Example – Segment #								
		1	2	3	4	5	6	7	8	9
Targets	Planning Cadence	Bi-Weekly	Bi-Weekly	Bi-Weekly	Weekly	Weekly	Weekly	Weekly	Weekly	Monthly
	% of SKUs	10%	5%	5%	15%	25%	15%	10%	10%	5%
	% of Revenue	10%	10%	5%	15%	30%	15%	5%	5%	5%
	% of Inventory	10%	5%	5%	15%	25%	15%	10%	10%	5%
	% of Planning Effort	25%	25%	25%	5%	5%	5%	5%	2%	3%
	Touch Level of Planners	High	High	High	Low	Low	Low	Low	Low	Low

Chart 8.13 Planning System Goals

means that we take the entire inventory database and run it through the logic flow, identifying into which segment each inventory item will fall. Then we look at the results of this distribution of inventory items and check the distribution of SKUs, the distribution of revenue, and the units of inventory distribution to see how close we came to our targets in Chart 8.13. Inevitably, we will need to do some tweaking, either to the model in Charts 8.9 and 8.10, or to our expectations in Chart 8.13. We also need to check the data. Often, in an attempt to get through this process quickly we will see data randomly inserted in the Master Data, and inaccurately inserted data will cause a misdistribution of the parts into incorrect segments. In this case, segmentation will not occur as desired because of the poor data. An iterative process occurs where we redistribute the parts repeatedly until we get the results we need in order to move forward with execution.

Execute

Within the execution phase, we move away from the analysis of the historical data and take a close look at the actual live data. We start planning and executing against the live inventory data. We use the results of the SCS process to improve our planning and scheduling and hopefully achieve the goals we outlined in Step 1 of Chart 8.3.

Looking at Step 8 of Chart 8.3, we grab the live data and run it through the logic flow of Chart 8.10. In Step 9, we look at the results of this exercise to see how well the current live data maps against the expectations that we highlighted in Chart 8.13. As always in the SCS process, we take a close look at the results and initiate appropriate corrective action, as identified in Step 10. Finally, we validate the overall performance of the SCS exercise in Step 11 by confirming that we have achieved the goals identified in Step 1.

Execution sounds simplistic, but in reality it is one of the most complex pieces of SCS because it requires all the effort of the SCS team including the business specialists who are focused on performance, the IT specialists who executed the segmentation through some customized IT process, and the analytics team that generates the performance metrics, which proves that the SCS worked or failed. When all of the parties involved feel that the breakdown of the segmentation structure is correct, and that the anticipated performance results have been achieved, that is the point where we can declare SCS a success.

Summary

In summary, we need to do a couple of things. The most important is to check whether you successfully solved the Planner's Nemesis of Chart 8.2. You can check your solution against Chart 8.14. The second item of importance is whether you are now comfortable with the flow of the SCS process and if you feel you can execute SCS for your own organization.

Chapter 8 drills more deeply into some of the conceptual issues that will be encountered as you try to use SCS. These conceptual issues involve various tools and their analytics and calculations. The intent of the chapter is not to provide

The Planner's Nemesis – Solution

Arrange the symbols so that you end up with
a row of alternating symbols in four moves,
moving two adjacent symbols in each move.

Chart 8.14 The Planner's Nemesis—Solution

you with a perfect understanding of these tools. Rather, it is trying to help you be ready for the inevitable number crunching issues that you will definitely encounter.

> If you talk to a man in a language he understands, that goes to his head. If you talk to him in his language, that goes to his heart.
>
> **Nelson Mandela**

9

SCS Key Concepts

If you're on a path with no obstacles, you're going nowhere.

This chapter will focus on several key concepts that are integral parts of using SCS in production or Supply Chain optimization. There is both Demand side segmentation as well as Supply side segmentation (see Chart 9.1). However, before we dive into a discussion of these concepts, let us retest our Planner Analytics skills. In Chart 9.2, we have buckets containing balls and we need to figure out how well the scheduling process works. Can you figure out how many balls are in each bucket?

While you are solving the bucket and ball mystery, let me refer you back to a chart you have seen in the last three

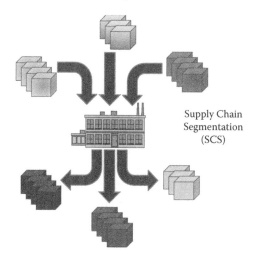

Supply Chain Segmentation (SCS)

Chart 9.1 SCS Segmentation

Balls in Buckets

We have 100 balls in 5 buckets.

Bucket # 1 plus Bucket # 2 has 52 balls.

Bucket # 2 plus Bucket # 3 has 43 balls.

Bucket # 3 plus Bucket # 4 has 34 balls.

Bucket # 4 plus Bucket # 5 has 30 balls.

How many balls are in each bucket?

Chart 9.2 Balls in a Bucket

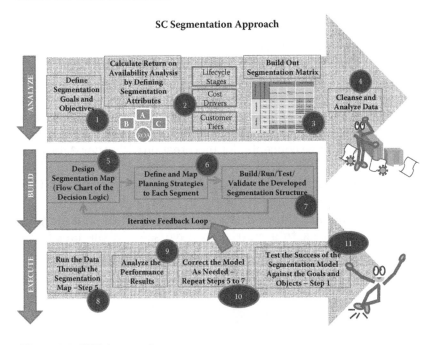

Chart 9.3 SCS Approach

chapters, now presented as Chart 9.3. The reason for introducing this chart again in this chapter is that we will be discussing a broad collection of SCS tools, and these tools will reflect back to various steps in this chart. As we attempt to perform a variety of calculations related to these charts, the tools listed in this chapter will pop up repeatedly and so it becomes important to be familiar with a few basic calculations. It becomes increasingly important when you try to integrate SCS with ERP software like SAP because the calculations within SAP are obscenely complex to the point of being ridiculous. For example, I recently worked a segmentation exercise with a company where several SAP consultants were also an integral part of the team. The reason for bringing them on the team was that we planned to build the segmentation structure into the SAP APO software and we found that even simple and basic calculations like the calculation for safety stock was so complex that the SAP consultants could not explain it, even after several phone calls with their corporate offices. The result was that we had to override the safety stock calculations and plug our own, spreadsheet-generated calculations into SAP so that we could get the desired results. Complexity is not helpful in these situations.

I will be referring to Chart 9.3 as I go through the following SCS key planning concepts. As you will see, several of the concepts fit into several of the steps in the model of Chart 9.3.

SCS Planning and Scheduling Key Concepts

Many concepts become relevant in the SCS process, and I am going to introduce them at this point because to have introduced them earlier would have made the discussion of SCS excessively complex. The following are basic planning and scheduling tools that are used throughout the production planning and Supply Chain planning and scheduling process. I need to introduce them because a user of SCS will eventually encounter them and should be familiar with them. This is not intended to be an in-depth or detailed discussion of these concepts. Rather, I will just be introducing them to you and you may need to go to other sources for more detailed information. The concepts are:

- Touch
- ERP Integration
- Life of a Product
- Forecast Analysis
- Statistical Safety Stock
- Optimal Service Level
- Coefficient of Variation

- Reorder Point Cycle
- EOQ
- OIL Planning
- Min/Max Planning
- BTO/MTO Planning
- EOL Planning

Touch

Although not stressed thus far in this book, numerous SCS systems are built around the concept of "touch." Touch can include things such as:

- The number of keystrokes on a computer
- The number of handwritten postings
- The number of times contact is made with a customer or a supplier
- The amount of effort required by a planner

Measuring the amount of touch can be a measure of waste. Excessive number of touches or an excessive amount of touch time means more work, longer cycle times, and more opportunities for errors. An example of a segmentation model based on touch can be seen in Chart 9.4.

In Chart 9.4, we see product lifecycle as one of the dimensions, volume as another, and variability as the third.

In the "touch" approach to SCS, there are numerous policy impacts to both the staffing and inventory levels. For example, in "No Touch" quadrants we automate everything, utilizing ERP for statistical forecasting, safety stock calculations, reorder point calculations, etc. The "High-Touch" quadrant requires collaborative forecasting, usually something like S&OP. Safety stock buffers tend to be higher, and information is less reliable. In the "Medium-Touch" quadrant, we are transitioning from "High-Touch" stability to less predictable declining or EOL products. We utilize automation such as ERP-based Min/Max calculations whenever possible.

When looking at production from a Push-Pull perspective, where Push is defined as when we "push" the product on the customer, and Pull is defined as when the customer "pulls" the

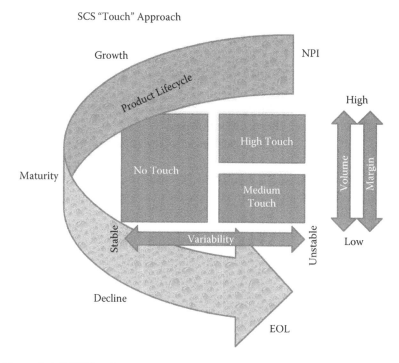

SCS "Touch" Approach

Chart 9.4 SCS Touch

product from us, High Touch is Push-based and Medium or Low Touch is Pull-based.

ERP Integration

SCS is nearly impossible to execute without some form of ERP. This is primarily because SCS is extremely data and analytics dependent. We need several years of order data to generate meaningful forecasts. We need Master Data that gives us information about customer tiers, lead times, product costs, etc. We need to execute the planning process through the ERP and the ERP needs to be flexible enough to allow us to use different planning tools based on a segment number.

The ERP tool we use needs to be able to interface with our segmentation tool, assuming it is external to the ERP environment. Another option is to build the segmentation tool into the ERP software. The information exchange will need to go both ways. The segmentation tool needs to pull data from the ERP. The types of data required include:

- Raw order and forecast data (cleansed from anomalies de-seasonalized or not)
- NPI initiation dates
- EOL product termination dates
- Coefficient of Variation/Variability measures

Similarly, the ERP needs to be able to accept overrides to the Materials Master from the segmentation tool for things like

- Segment number
- Safety stock
- Service level

This is especially important in those cases where the ERP environment does not produce the answers that we find acceptable (which, unfortunately, occurs far too often).

Life of a Product

An exercise that is invaluable when you work through the SPS process is the analysis of the Life of a Product. What we are doing here is defining the product lifecycle stages and focusing on the characteristics that define each of these stages. For example, when do we have enough information and history to decide if a product has moved from the NPI stage into the Growth stage? What do we need to know so we can automate the planning process for this product? Is the NPI stage the same for all our products? For example, in Chart 9.5 we see an example where an NPI is the replacement product for an existing product, and rather than going through an S&OP exercise we can move this product directly to Growth or Maturity stages because of the reliable history from the product being replaced.

Similarly, we need to think through the transitions between all the different stages. What are the characteristics of each stage? What piece of data do we need in order to determine that a transition has occurred between the stages?

The Life of a Product

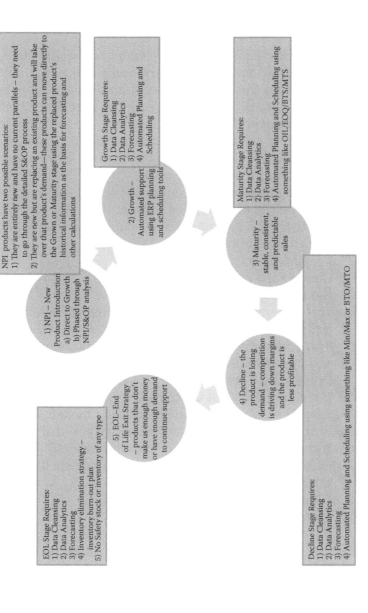

NPI products have two possible scenarios:
1) They are entirely new and have no current parallels – they need to go through the detailed S&OP process
2) They are new but are replacing an existing product and will take over that product's demand—these products can move directly to the Grown or Maturity stage using the replaced product's historical information as the basis for forecasting and other calculations

Growth Stage Requires:
1) Data Cleansing
2) Data Analytics
3) Forecasting
4) Automated Planning and Scheduling

Maturity Stage Requires:
1) Data Cleansing
2) Data Analytics
3) Forecasting
4) Automated Planning and Scheduling using something like OIL/EOQ/BTS/MTS

2) Growth – Automated support using ERP planning and scheduling tools

1) NPI – New Product Introduction
a) Direct to Growth
b) Phased through NPI/S&OP analysis

3) Maturity – stable, consistent, and predictable sales

4) Decline – the product is losing demand – competition is driving down margins and the product is less profitable

5) EOL–End of Life Exit Strategy – products that don't make us enough money or have enough demand to continue support

EOL Stage Requires:
1) Data Cleansing
2) Data Analytics
3) Forecasting
4) Inventory elimination strategy – inventory burn-out plan
5) No Safety stock or inventory of any type

Decline Stage Requires:
1) Data Cleansing
2) Data Analytics
3) Forecasting
4) Automated Planning and Scheduling using something like Min/Max or BTO/MTO

Chart 9.5 The Life of a Product

Forecast Analysis

I am not going to give a detailed discussion of forecasting, but I am going to highlight some key points that seem to be missed when going through an SCS exercise. Here are some basic rules:

a. Forecast data should be based on orders, not on shipments.
b. Forecast data based on the originally requested customer date for the order is better than the negotiated or agreed upon date (which often includes a lot of reschedules and recommits).
c. Forecast data contains errors and anomalies, like sales promotions, and this needs to be cleansed if we are to get a meaningful set of forecasts.
d. Forecasting requires the removal of seasonality, which can only be calculated if you have at least two years of data. Otherwise, seasonal trends cannot be calculated. This may be a problem in some forecasts.
e. The steps in forecasting should be:
    1. Cleanse the data.
    2. Remove seasonality.
    3. Test a variety of forecasting models and validate them by using some error calculator and then select the best model (the one exhibiting the least amount of error) and use this model to project your future forecast.
    4. Project the forecast.
    5. Put seasonality back into the results.
f. When considering different forecasting models, amazingly the simplistic (time series) often perform better than the complex (like associative forecasting). Do not forget to try out the simple time series models like:
    1. Simple moving average
    2. Weighted moving average
    3. Exponential smoothing
    4. Regression
g. If the ERP software you are using does not allow these simple steps, than I would strongly recommend you do the forecasting off-line, possibly even with a spreadsheet, because you will get better results. Sadly, some of the available ERPs are so wrapped up in their sophistication that it encumbers the simplistic.

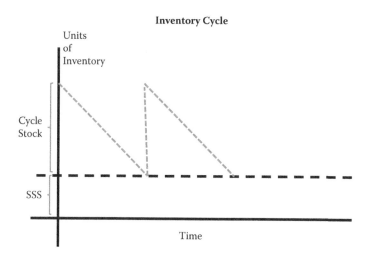

Chart 9.6 Inventory Cycle

Statistical Safety Stock (SSS)

Once again, there is no standard calculation for SSS. However, I will suggest a calculation that I feel works best for my purposes. The logic behind SSS is that you have a buffer of inventory that will protect you in the event that you run out of your cycle inventory (inventory actively used in the process, which is used up and replaced). The intent is that if you hit the point where you have used up your cycle inventory and you do not have an active order, you should be able to place an order and receive the order before you completely run out of inventory (see Chart 9.6). Therefore, SSS should contain the amount of inventory you use up (on the average) during the ordering lead time.

In addition, a variability component needs to be included in SSS. Depending on the lack of stability of the inventory burn-off, we would order a number of standard deviations of additional buffer material to satisfactorily cover the inventory fluctuations based on the service level we plan to provide. The result of all this is the following formula:

$$SSS = (\text{average daily usage}) \times (\text{order lead time in days})$$
$$+ (\text{Z factor}) \times \sqrt{(\text{Daily Usage}^2 \times \text{Standard Deviation}^2)}$$
$$= (\text{Demand/Days Worked}) \times (\text{Order Lead Time}) + (\text{Z factor})$$
$$\times \sqrt{(((\text{Demand/Days Worked})^2) \times (\text{Standard Deviation}^2)}$$

Z Factor Table

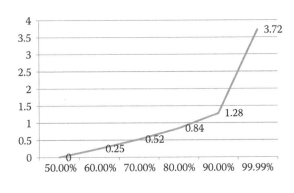

Service Level	Service Factor
50.00%	0
60.00%	0.25
70.00%	0.52
80.00%	0.84
85.00%	1.04
90.00%	1.28
92.00%	1.41
94.00%	1.55
96.00%	1.75
98.00%	2.05
99.00%	2.33
99.50%	2.58
99.70%	2.75
99.90%	3.09
99.99%	3.72

Chart 9.7 Z-Factor Table

The Z factor is tied directly to the service level that we are planning to achieve. A brief table of Z factors can be seen in Chart 9.7. From this table you can see how dramatically the Z factor multiplies the amount of SSS as we increase the desired service level.

In the formula, one standard deviation of inventory is a calculation of the standard deviation based on order history. This is the quantity of inventory covered by one standard deviation.

Optimal Service Level (OSL)

The calculation of OSL is hotly debated, and if you go to the Internet, you will find a plethora of options. Service level calculations become important because they directly affect the level of safety stock and therefore inventory costs. Fundamentally, service level is about stock-out avoidance. It is a balancing act among how much inventory we should carry, what the corresponding cost of that inventory is, and how many stock-outs we should expect at that inventory level. Therefore, we are asking

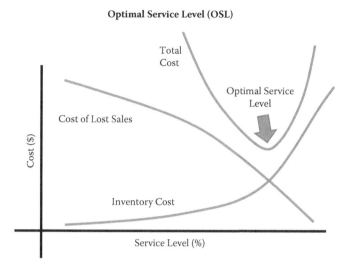

Optimal Service Level (OSL)

Chart 9.8 OSL

ourselves the question, "At what point is the margin that we are earning on the product no longer worth the inventory cost that it will cost us to achieve that one extra product sale?" We want to know the level at which the inventory-related costs are the same as the cost of lost sales.

OSL is used to help us achieve the largest number of sales at the least amount of cost. Increasing service level demands higher inventory, which triggers higher inventory cost. Increased inventory reduces the possibility of losing sales. As a result, the cost of lost sales decreases. In Chart 9.8, we see that OSL is the point where total cost is minimized.

The formulas are (of course, there are several options for these calculations, but I am just trying to introduce the concept in this book and then it requires the reader's effort to attempt to customize this for his or her specific application):

Inventory Cost = Holding Cost × Statistical Safety Stock

Cost of Lost Sales = Margin × (Difference between the Z factor of OSL and the Z factor of the target service level[2]) × (Demand per day) = Margin × (((Z factor at 99.99% service level, which is 3.72) − (Z factor at the target service level))[2]) × ((Annual Demand)/(Days Worked))

Optimal Service Level (OSL) Example

Service Level	Inventory Cost	Cost of Lost Sales	Total Cost
60.00%	1284	42143	43428
70.00%	2749	35840	38589
80.00%	4588	29030	33618
85.00%	5795	25138	30933
90.00%	7301	20838	28139
92.00%	8143	18676	26820
94.00%	9071	16481	25553
96.00%	10434	13583	24018
98.00%	12561	9761	22323
99.00%	14636	6762	21398
99.50%	16561	4549	21110
99.70%	17909	3293	21203
99.90%	20701	1389	22091
99.99%	26211	0	26211

Chart 9.9 OSL Example

Inventory Cost is primarily focused on SSS, which is a variable that is geometrically growing based on service level, and which in turn drives up inventory cost as service level increases.

Cost of lost sales is inversely proportional to service level and decreases as service level increases because fewer sales are missed.

A graphical example of OSL can be seen in Chart 9.9, where the low point in the Total Cost curve indicates the OSL. (This graph is somewhat out of scale because the intervals to the right of the graph are closer together than on the left—the interval spacing is not the same all the way across—but it demonstrates how OSL would be used.)

OSL is a key driver in the calculation of SSS. It recommends a level of service that would financially be the most beneficial solution for this particular product. Then, using this OSL-derived SSS number we can press forward and calculate the OIL, which is one of the planning tools that we have been referencing in this book.

Coefficient of Variation (CoV)

CoV (not to be confused with covariance, which is entirely different) is defined as the ratio of standard deviation to mean.

It measures the variability of a data series. This is a key metric when we are trying to determine product stability. Without some level of product stability, it is difficult to automate the planning and scheduling process.

CoV is used to measure variability of demand for any particular SKU. CoV has an advantage over Standard Deviation, which is the more popular measure of variability because in CoV the variations are always with respect to the mean. The standard deviation of two different data series cannot be meaningfully compared. However, CoV of those two series indicates the variation of the values around each respective mean.

A CoV of less than 1 suggests that the product history is relatively stable and therefore reasonably predictable. Hence, products with a demand profile that results in a CoV of less than 1 suggests that these products are easier to forecast compared to the rest. Similarly, a CoV of more than 1 indicates that the series is relatively unstable and forecasting future demand based on historical data is less reliable.

The calculation of CoV requires at least three non-zero data points. Otherwise, with only two or one data point the CoV calculation is meaningless.

The formula for CoV is:

$$CoV = Standard\ Deviation/Mean$$

Reorder Point Cycle (ROP)

ROP is the inventory level at which a replacement order is triggered. As inventory is used up, inventory level is monitored, and when we hit the ROP level of inventory, the system automatically places a replenishment order.

ROP is calculated by the following formula:

$$ROP = SSS + (days\ of\ lead\ time) \times (averaged\ daily\ usage)$$

In Chart 9.10, we see a typical example of ROP. When our inventory level hits the SSS level, the order that was placed earlier when we hit the ROP level arrives. When the order arrives, it replenishes our inventory back up to its maximum level.

ROP is a basic inventory stock replenishment methodology that is used in several automated planning processes.

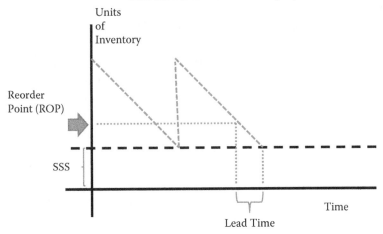

Chart 9.10 Reorder Point

Economic Order Quantity (EOQ)

EOQ is a foundational tool from which most of the current planning and scheduling methodologies were derived. For example, MRP uses EOQ ROP for its planning options. JIT inventory planning uses EOQ to calculate Kanban size. OIL is just a relabeling of the EOQ philosophy with some minor enhancements. Therefore, a clear understanding of the EOQ concept is fundamental in understanding most of the other concepts, which are just derivatives of EOQ and use it as their foundation.

The basic principle behind EOQ is that it attempts to minimize the Total Cost of Inventory. Within the EOQ structure, there are three inventory cost components:

Fixed Cost
Ordering Cost
Carrying Cost

The fundamental formula looks like this:

$$\text{Total Cost (TC)} = \text{Fixed Cost (FC)}$$

$$+ \text{Ordering Cost (OC)} + \text{Carrying Cost (CC)}$$

where:

$$FC = SSS \times (\text{Carrying Cost Rate } (C_R))$$

$$OC = (\text{Number of Orders Placed } (N)) \times (\text{Cost Per Order } (C_O))$$

$$CC = (\text{Average Inventory Level } (A)) \times (\text{Carrying Cost Rate } (C_R))$$

The final formula is:

$$TC = SSS \times C_R + N \times C_O + A \times C_R$$

where:

$$N = (\text{Demand } (D))/(\text{Order Size } (Q))$$

$$A = (\text{Order Size } (Q))/2$$

The resulting formula is:

$$TC = SSS \times C_R + (D/Q) \times C_O + (Q/2) \times C_R$$

Solving for the minimal TC requires taking the first derivative of the TC equation and setting it equal to zero. Alternatively, we can get the same result if we realize that the FC component does not vary and therefore is irrelevant in the calculation, and that we are looking for the point where OC = CC. The result is the formula:

$$OC = CC$$

$$(D/Q) \times C_O = (Q/2) \times C_R$$

Reshuffling the terms gives us:

$$Q^2 = (2 \times D \times C_O)/(C_R)$$

Or, the preferred version:

$$Q = \sqrt{((2 \times D \times C_O)/(C_R))}$$

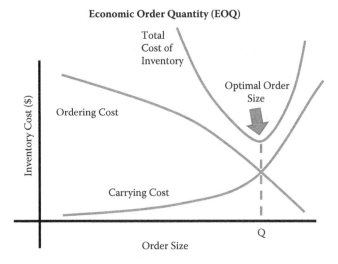

Economic Order Quantity (EOQ)

Chart 9.11 EOQ

The graph for this model can be seen in Chart 9.11, where we see OC decreasing as the order size increases because we order less frequently, and CC increasing as the order size increases because the average amount of inventory that we carry in stock increases. The resulting Optimal Order Size (Q) occurs when the Total Cost of Inventory is minimized. Looking back at Chart 9.10, the size (height) of the saw tooth (the difference between SSS and the peak of the tooth) is equal to Q.

Optimal Inventory Level (OIL)

The objective behind OIL is to identify the most optimal stocking level for your overall inventory planning systems. It is the integration of many of the principles we have already discussed in this chapter. It starts by identifying the best possible forecast for a product, using data cleansing, depersonalization, and de-trending techniques. The objective is to get as flat and straight a line as possible so that the forecast projection is as accurate as possible. Then we reinsert the trend and seasonal information into the data to identify our true forecast.

Next, we utilize service level information to generate an SSS. Then, using EOQ we calculate the optimal order size, and using order lead time we calculate ROP. We now know when to order and how much to order, and we can calculate the Total Cost of Inventory (TC).

When validating that OIL generates better results than what you were previously achieving, we need to look at:

Number of Stock-outs
Total Cost of Inventory
Number of On-Time Deliveries

By considering all these metrics, we can receive an accurate determination if OIL is outperforming the previous tools that you were using for planning and scheduling. Amazingly, we often find that a simple tool like OIL performs much better than any other system in an environment of low forecast variability and high volume.

Min/Max (MM) Planning

Min/Max (MM) is a system that takes OIL and puts limits on the SSS and Q levels. It is primarily used when the product's demand is decaying. During declining demand, a product starts to lose its order stability. Orders become more sporadic and forecasts are less reliable. In these situations, the SSS automatically starts to grow to cover the variability. Therefore, an organization systematically decides to reduce product availability and product service level. The company would put caps on the levels of SSS and Maximum Inventory (MI) levels (MI = SSS + Q as seen in our previous discussions). For example, the Min level of inventory (which replaces our SSS and becomes an override for SSS) is often set at the total of the forecasted demand over the acquisition lead time (the time it takes to receive that demand or Average Forecast per week times the lead time in weeks). The Max level of inventory is also set based on a factor of the forecasted demand over lead time. A common factor would be to double Min (Max = 2 × Min). However, as the product variability continues to increase which is demonstrated by showing that the covariance (CoV) increases, we may want to make the Max equal to 2.5 times the Min as a greater protective buffer. The risk we are taking is that we are increasing our level of average inventory as we do this and it becomes possible that we will be left with obsolete inventory.

The process is that whenever the inventory level hits Min, we place an order to replenish our inventory back up to Max by ordering Max items, and by the time we run out of stock the replacement order will arrive "Lead Time" days later and replenish us to this desired level of inventory. The Min level acts as an ROP.

Build to Order (BTO)/Manufacture to Order (MTO) Planning

At some point, we will determine that a product is no longer profitable and that we want to start to phase out our support of the product. We decide that the service level is irrelevant. We determine that the additional lead time that we require to order the manufacture of the product will now be added to the lead time that we present as the total product lead time for our customers. We only order the product when we have a firm customer order in hand, and then we order what we need to specifically satisfy that customer order and no more. There is no automated replenishment process. Ordering is easy because it is directly dependent on the customer orders.

End of Life (EOL) Planning

EOL is just as it states. We are planning to terminate the product from our offerings. We have some remaining inventory that we are planning to burn off as orders come in, but we will not be producing any more of that product in the future. Therefore, when stock runs out, we are done with the product. In this case, we will receive customer orders, and fill those orders out of existing inventory as long as available inventory exists. We also set a product termination date, which tells us that after this date we will no longer offer this product and we will scrap any remaining units that we have left of this product.

The difference between BTO and EOL is that in BTO, we still generate a forecast and the forecast is used in determining the Min and Max values. In EOL, we have decided not to buy any more inventory and we only want to burn up the inventory we already have whereas in BTO we still place production orders to replenish the product.

Summary

This chapter has focused on several key production planning concepts that are integral parts of using SCS in production or Supply Chain optimization. We learned about several different tools that are generally applied at the various lifecycle stages of a product. At each stage, a different planning tool is used to optimize the cost of inventory at that level. This will help you after you have defined your segments and are looking to match the tool to the segment.

Before we leave this chapter, we need to see how well you performed on my test of your Planner Analytics skills. In Chart 9.12, you see the results of the test where we have buckets containing balls and we needed to figure out how well our scheduling process works. How close did you come to figuring out how many balls are in each bucket?

Hard work never killed a man
But it sure scared a lot of them

Balls in Buckets – Solution

We have 100 balls in 5 buckets.

Bucket # 1 plus Bucket # 2 has 52 balls.

Bucket # 2 plus Bucket # 3 has 43 balls.

Bucket # 3 plus Bucket # 4 has 34 balls.

Bucket # 4 plus Bucket # 5 has 30 balls.

How many balls are in each Bucket?

Answers: 1–27, 2–25, 3–18, 4–16, 5–14

Chart 9.12 Balls in a Bucket—Solution

SECTION 3

Segmentation Effects

10
Change Management

By failing to prepare, you are preparing to fail.

Benjamin Franklin

The business functions of an organization have, for a long time, focused on stability rather than on change. Chart 10.1 re-emphasizes that change will occur when segmentation is introduced. For example, accounting, finance, personnel, the legal department, most upper management, and marketing would love nothing more than to have steady, stable growth. Operations, traditionally, would love a perfectly balanced operation with just the right amount of inventory, just the right workforce, and no problems. However, one of the competitive lessons we have learned is that stability breeds failure. If we try to stay where we are, we will be run over. Change happens to us whether we like it or not. The climate changes, competition changes, the market changes, etc. Optimizing a Supply Chain is the process of optimizing a continuously changing environment.

Supply Chain Segmentation (SCS) and Change

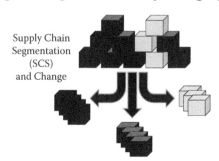

Chart 10.1 SCS and Change

We have learned the new competitive lesson that the only way to competitive success is through change management.

The function of the organization has changed from one of seeking stability to one of managing change—change in products and their components, change in demand, changes in resources and their availability, changes in operational technology, changes in competitive product makeup, changes in competition, etc. Continuous improvement (change) is critical in a global economy. Changes should include:

Product innovation
Process innovation (what the Japanese are good at)
Technology innovation
Time-to-market innovation (Taiwan)
Marketing innovation

Uncontrolled and undirected change can be as disastrous as no change. What we need is to be able to stay ahead of the change curve. We need to change ourselves faster than external forces have a chance to change us. We need the change to be focused on a target. Moreover, we need to maintain our corporate integrity as we institute change.

To manage change we need to incorporate change models into our business that facilitate the change process. Some of these change models, such as Total Quality Management (TQM) and Process Re-engineering (PR), have had success in the past and many organizations still swear by them. Today we are looking at additional tools like Lean and Six Sigma.

Most change models contain some label of quality in them. Quality has become the flag behind which the battle for continuous change is most often fought. However, "quality" does not fully define everything that is wanted by the change process. Nevertheless, terms like TQM and Quality Functional Deployment (QFD) are change processes that look like they focus on quality. However, in reality, like all change models they focus on positive goal direct changes in all the measurement areas including quality, productivity, efficiency, financial improvements, etc. In this chapter, we will initially only discuss and compare the extremes in how change should be implemented. We will compare two change models: TQM and PR.

The focus of any change model should be on continuous improvement in the broad sense, which includes both the Japanese incremental step perspective and the U.S. break-through business process improvement perspective. The need for change is rarely argued. What is different between the various change models is the speed of the change and the depth at which the change occurs. This is where the Japanese and the U.S. change methods bump heads. In comparison, the U.S. model entails:

Fast change.
Fast return on investment.
Radical and dramatic change.
Deep and extensive changes feeling the need to redefine the whole process.
On the hunt for the one big change that will fix all the problems.
PR, which is characterized by rapid/radical changes and focuses on change implementation and high-tech solutions.
Slower to get around to making any change because the change process is viewed as being so extensive, dramatic, and upsetting. The result is that there is more resistance to any change process.
Change ownership belongs to some change "hero" who quite often is the CEO.

The Japanese model entails:

Slow change.
Long-term return on investments.
Carefully planned out changes.
Think the change through carefully.
Plan before you implement.
Small step changes.
TQM, which focuses on analysis and planning in the change process and technology-that-fits-the-situation solutions.

The change process is much less painful because change involves small, un-dramatic steps. Therefore, there is much less resistance and step-wise, small changes are continuously occurring.

Change ownership is shared.

> Einstein was asked, if he had 60 minutes left in which to save the world, what would he do. His answer was that he would spend 55 minutes planning, and 5 minutes implementing.

Some methodologies have attempted, unsuccessfully, to combine the Japanese and U.S. approaches by suggesting the implementation of radical changes without being radical. What they are hoping to do is implement big changes without upsetting the entire organization and developing enormous resistance to the change process. However, no one has come up with a good way to accomplish this (probably because no one really understands it). Therefore, the conflict between the two change approaches remains. TQM continues to be viewed as "too slow" by the United States, and PR continues to be viewed as "too destructive" by the Japanese.

Let us now consider several of the most popular models for change and discuss the procedures used in implementing these models. We will consider:

QFD
TQM
PR
Concept Management (CM)
Lean
Six Sigma

Some of these models only supply us with focus areas of improvement. Others have specific procedures for the change process. The models should not be thought of as exclusive in that if you pick one you could not use any of the others. Rather, they should all be considered as stepping stones toward the development of a successful change program. Depending on the change that we are implementing, one change methodology may be more effective than the other may be.

Quality Functional Deployment (QFD)

QFD is the implementation of a continuous improvement process focusing on the customer. It was developed at Mitsubishi's Kobe Shipyards and focuses on directing the efforts of all functional areas on a common goal. In Mitsubishi's case, the goal was "satisfying the needs of the customer." Several changes were instituted in order to accomplish this, such as increased horizontal communication within the company. One of the most immediate results was a reduced time-to-market lead time for products.

QFD systematizes the product's attributes in a matrix diagram called a house of quality and highlights which of these attributes is the most important to a customer. This helps the teams throughout the organization focus on their goal (customer satisfaction) whenever they are making change decisions.

QFD focuses on:

1. The customer
2. Systemizing the customer satisfaction process by developing a matrix for defining:
   a. Customer quality
   b. Product characteristics
   c. Process characteristics
   d. Process control characteristics
3. Empowered teaming
4. Extensive front-end analysis, which involves 14 steps in defining the "house of quality"
   a. Create and communicate a project objective
   b. Establish the scope of the project
   c. Obtain customer requirements
   d. Categorize customer requirements
   e. Prioritize customer requirements
   f. Assess competitive position
   g. Develop design requirements
   h. Determine relationship between design requirements and customer requirements

i. Assess competitive position in terms of design requirements
j. Calculate importance of design requirements
k. Establish target values for design
l. Determine correlations between design requirements
m. Finalize target values for design
n. Develop the other matrices

Implementing and using QFD is not an easy process. A great deal of commitment throughout the company is required for the process to be successful. The results of effective implementation are well worth the effort. Reduced product development time, increased flexibility, increased customer satisfaction, and lower start-up costs are just a few of the benefits that can be expected through the use of QFD.

Gregg D. Stocker

QFD has been widely recognized as an effective tool for focusing the product and the process on customer satisfaction. Much has been written on the subject. However, as discussed earlier, QFD is a Japanese approach to focused change and therefore focuses on extensive analysis, utilizing the philosophy that we need to make sure we are doing the right things, before we worry about doing things right!

Detailed analysis through the matrices is time consuming, conceptual planning time is much extended by QFD. However, the overall design-to-market time should be cut because the design effort focuses on the most important areas.

Dave Henrickson

Total Quality Management (TQM)

Simply put, TQM is a management approach to long-term customer satisfaction. TQM is based on the participation of all members of an organization in improving the processes, products, services and the culture they work in.

Karen Bemkowski

As mentioned earlier, TQM focuses on careful, thoughtful analysis. However, the analysis should be creative, innovative, and innoveering oriented. The carefulness comes in when it comes time to implement. We want to make sure that we are implementing positive, goal-focused changes before we move a muscle.

TQM is much broader than QFD. TQM is a change model that is enterprise-wide. Some people define TQM in general terms as simply making the entire organization responsible for product or service quality. This is the way TQM is defined in many organizations and it encompasses everything and anything. However, there is also a specific, proceduralistic version of the definition of TQM. Perhaps the best way to understand TQM is to look at the TQM process. After, we can consider the significance of TQM and its process.

TQM is not just a tool; it has an entire philosophy about how businesses should be run. The philosophy of TQM is filled with ideas and attitudes, like:

Desiring and searching out change
Think culture—move from copying to innovating
Do the right things before you do things right
Focus on the goal
Measurement/motivation planning
Top to bottom corporate strategy
Company-wide involvement
Clear definition and implementation of quality
Education, training, and cross training
Integration and coordination
Small, step-by-step improvements

In TQM, the philosophy behind change is that we become excited about changes. We look for opportunity to change, especially because change should mean that we are becoming better. To be a TQM organization is to become an organization that wants to be the best and realizes that there is always room for improvement.

In operationalizing TQM, there are several points of importance. They are:

The TQM Coordinating Team (Quality Council)
The Three P Teams—Cross-Functional Teams
The TQM Project Implementation Steps

Training Programs
Measurement and Feedback
Showcasing
Team Building
Systematic Problem Solving (SPS)

TQM implementations start with a coordinating team, often referred to as a Quality Council. This is a team composed of high-level corporate leaders from all functional areas. This team is appointed by the CEO and operates under his or her direction. The CEO takes an active part in directing the activities of the team. This Quality Council is then responsible for organizing and measuring the performance of the other TQM teams within the organization. It oversees the installation, training, performance, and measurement of the other teams. This team focuses specifically on the corporate goal and definition of quality.

The Quality Council will organize three different types of teams referred to as the cross-functional three P teams. These teams are process, product, and project teams. The process teams are ongoing, continuous improvement teams set up at different levels of the organization. They look for improvements in the organization's functioning processes. These teams should be composed of both "insiders" and "outsiders." The insiders know and understand existing functions and operations. The outsiders challenge the status quo.

The second of the three P teams are the product teams. These teams are cross functional but focus on a specific product, product line, or service. They are customer and vendor interface teams that are specifically oriented toward the development of new products and the improvement of existing products. Their life span is the same as the life span of the product they represent.

The third of the three P teams are the project teams. These teams are limited life teams set up to specifically focus on a specific project, like the construction of a new plant or a computer installation. These teams may be the result of a specific process or product that is being targeted, or they may be set up to research something that the general management team is interested in developing or improving.

The TQM project implementation steps are as follows:

Identify problems (opportunities)
Prioritize these problems
Select the biggest bang-for-the-buck project
Develop an implementation plan
Use operations research and MIS tools where appropriate
Develop guideposts and an appropriate measurement system
Training
Implementation
Feedback—Monitoring—Control—Change
After successful project implementation and ongoing status,
    repeat cycle

The first function of the team is to identify its function and charter. If you are one of the three P teams, your team's charter is laid out for you by the Quality Council. If you are the Quality Council, this charter is laid out for you by the CEO and is aimed at the focused goals of the organization. After understanding its charter, the team then searches for and identifies problems that exist and that prevent the organization from achieving this charter. The word "problems" has a negative connotation. A better wording would be to say that we search for opportunities for improvements. We are not just trying to correct negative effects, we are looking for techniques or tools that will allow us to become better and possibly even best.

Next, we take these problems (opportunities) and prioritize them based on their effect on the charter of the team (which should be focused on the goals of the organization). We do a type of ABC analysis (80-20 Rule or Pareto Principle) to determine which change would have the greatest effect. Then we select the biggest bang-for-the-buck project and develop an implementation plan for this project. This implementation plan needs to contain guideposts that are based on an appropriate measurement system that points the team toward achieving its charter. The book *Breakthrough Thinking* does an excellent job of discussing opportunity identification techniques.*

---

* Nadler, Gerald and Shozo Hibino, *Breakthrough Thinking,* Prima Publishing and Communications, Rocklin, CA, 1990.
Nadler, Gerald, Shozo Hibino, and John Farrell, *Creative Solution Finding*, Prima Publishing and Communications, Rocklin, CA, 1995.

Training of the implementers and users is critical or else the planned project is doomed to failure. This training makes future users comfortable with the changes. It also offers a bit of ownership because the planned users will now feel comfortable with the changes.

The next step is implementation. The implementation should be a trivial process, if all the planning and training steps are performed carefully. Part of the implementation is the installation of feedback, monitoring, and control mechanisms, as laid out in the implementation plan. Careful monitoring allows corrective changes to occur whenever necessary.

After successful project implementation, and seeing that the ongoing status of the project is functioning correctly, the team repeats the implementation cycle, looking for more opportunities for change. If this process is performed correctly, the list of change opportunities should become longer with each iterative cycle. This means that your team is now open for newer and broader opportunities for change.

Training programs need to exist before and after project selection. In the before case, the TQM team needs to understand what tools are available to it. This training would involve an understanding of tools and techniques. Initial training could include programs in areas like operations research/management science tools and techniques, motivational/philosophical training, semi-technical and technical education, the operation of the systems approach, etc.

Training programs after TQM team implementation should be user training focused on the changes being implemented. These programs need to be defined (and often conducted) by the TQM team, which has the best understanding of the change.

The issue of measurement and feedback has already been discussed in Chapter 3. It is critical to realize the motivational role of the measurement system and that the proper implementation of an effective feedback (reporting) mechanism will assure the ongoing success of the changes implemented.

Showcasing is one of the best techniques for expanding implementation time. We use the Quality Council to develop and implement a "sure thing" TQM implementation project. We are attempting to demonstrate the successes of an organization-wide TQM implementation. In the United States, where short-term, quick benefits need to be demonstrated, show-casing becomes a critical part of the selling job of TQM.

There are several types of teams required in a TQM environment, like the Quality Council and the three P teams. Understanding which teams need to be organized is just a small part of the problem of team construction. A much bigger problem is making the team effective. For example, team training and team relationship building are necessary for effective interaction and for the synergy of the team.

TQM was the first stage of realizing that we need to take "quality" (or the search for positive change) out of the quality department and make it a company-wide program. TQM is a strategy toward continuous, corporate-wide change, it is a philosophy, it is an operationalized process, and it is a fad. It becomes a fad if we expect quick results and become disenchanted because we are not "like the Japanese" in the first two months. TQM is a strategy toward becoming leading edge and world class.

In spite of its slowness, TQM has been extremely successful internationally and is getting ever-increasing attention. TQM is a very specific process improvement step in a drive toward world-class status.

Process Re-Engineering

Wisely, and slowly. They stumble that run fast.

William Shakespeare, *Romeo and Juliet*

Process Re-Engineering (PR) is rapid, radical change. It is not downsizing, which many companies are using it for; rather, it is work elimination. It is positive, growth-focused change, looking for opportunities to eliminate waste and improve value added productivity, often through the implementation of technology.

However, just like any tool, some extremely positive aspects to PR make it worthy of our attention. The first is that PR focuses on change implementation at the top of the corporate hierarchy. It generates more of a top-down change culture. In addition, it focuses on process-oriented changes.

PR's focus on the process emphasizes that the process, not the products, holds the secrets for the most dramatic improvements within an organization. PR focuses on an all-or-nothing proposition that produces impressive results. PR is defined as:

> The fundamental rethinking and radical redesign of business processes to achieve dramatic improvements in critical, contemporary measures of performance, such as cost, quality, service, and speed.

The principles of PR include:

Organize around outcomes, not tasks.
Have those who use the output of the process perform the process.
Subsume information-processing work into the real work that produces information.
Treat geographically dispersed resources as though they were centralized.
Link parallel activities instead of integrating their results.
Put the decision point where the work is performed, and build control into the process.
Capture information once and at the source.

The three Rs of PR are:

Rethink—Is what you are doing focused on the customer?
Redesign—What are you doing? Should you be doing it at all? Redesign how it can be done.
Re-tool—Re-evaluate the use of advanced technologies.

Some characteristics of PR include:

Several jobs are combined into one.
Workers make the decisions—empowerment.
"Natural Order" sequencing of job steps.
Processes with multiple versions depending on the need.
Work is performed where it makes the most sense.
Checks and controls are reduced.
Reconciliation is minimized.
"Empowered" customer service representative.
Hybrid centralized/decentralized organizations.

Like TQM, the focus of the PR effort is the team. Empowered process teams replace departments. Executives change their role from scorekeeper to leader. Organizational structures become flatter. Managers change from supervisors to coaches.

PR has the following steps or phases in the change management process:

1. Mobilization
   Develop a vision
   Communicate the vision
   Identify champions and process owners
   Assemble the teams
2. Diagnosis
   Train and educate
   Current process analysis
   Select and scope the process
   Understand the current customer
   Model the process
   Identify problems
   Set targets for new designs
3. Redesign
   Create breakthrough design concepts
   Redesign the entire system
   Build prototype
   Information technology
4. Transition
   Finalize transition design
   Implementation phase
   Measure benefits
   The role of communication to avoid resistance
   You cannot over-communicate

PR has many of the procedural characteristics of TQM; however, it is more focused on speed than TQM. PR focuses on being competitive via the rapid and the radical, and it stresses the process as the key to successful change. Numerous books available discuss the philosophy of PR. The best is still the original, by the gurus of PR, Hammer and Champy.

Concept Management

Concept Management (CM) is another change model that comes from Japan and integrates TQM and World Class Management (WCM) principles into a change management process. CM is a Japanese movement that integrates Breakthrough Thinking (BT), WCM, and TQM. BT is the technique utilized to develop ideas. It moves away from the slowness and costliness of traditional root cause analysis commonly used in the United States and Europe. WCM offers the formal structure around which the ideas are turned into goals and a measurement/motivation system. TQM is the process for team-based idea/change implementation.

CM is an idea generation and implementation process used by companies like Toyota and Sony that breaks us out of the traditional, analytical thinking common to companies. Instead, it focuses on forming a purpose hierarchy through a series of steps.

CM uses the term "concept" to mean innovative purpose-driven change creation. It uses "management" to mean leadership. Therefore, CM is "innovative, change-oriented, purpose-driven (goal focused), creative leadership" (Plenert and Hibino, 1997). This leadership occurs through the integration of ideas, primarily the ideas expressed in two leading edge philosophies: BT and WCM.

Gerald Nadler and Shozo Hibino published *Breakthrough Thinking* and *Creative Solution Finding*. In these two books, they described a "Paradigm Shift in Thinking" called "Breakthrough Thinking." They explain how thinking paradigms have shifted over our history. They use the examples of Primitive, Early Greek, Classical Greek, God Thinking, Descartes, etc. Our thinking paradigms have been continuously shifting over time. Our conventional thinking paradigm (Descartes Thinking) is out of date with a rapidly changing world and needs to shift again to a new thinking paradigm, BT. In the future, we have to be Multi-Thinkers who are able to use all three thinking paradigms: God Thinking, Conventional (Descartes) Thinking, and BT.

The three thinking paradigms are completely different and each has a different approach. We cannot neglect any of these three thinking paradigms because each has an influence in the decision-making process. We have to select and utilize each of these paradigms on a case-by-case basis. Someone who uses and interchanges these thinking paradigms is referred to as a "Multi-Thinker."

WCM is broad in its application, and numerous publications discuss the subject in detail (see Plenert's books *World Class Manager* and *Making Innovation Happen: Concept Management through Integration*). However, in order to get a clear understanding of how WCM manages change, the focus would be on:

1. People—Employees and stakeholders are the source of change opportunities. They need to be motivated properly through an appropriate measurement system in order to drive change.
2. Customers—Customers are the reason for change. In order to be competitive, we need to give our customers a clear reason why they should not buy from anyone else but us.
3. Performance—Performance requires focus on a goal, whether it is financial, quality, or some other focus. Then we need to measure, monitor, and offer feedback information about our performance.
4. Competitors—Competition creates fear, but it also creates opportunity. Competitors need to be analyzed and understood in order to be defeated.
5. Future—The future is coming whether we are ready for it or not. If we are not ready for it, it will pass us by, along with our customers and competitors.
6. Integration—Through integration, everyone and everything work together. Managers are not merely bosses; they are leaders and facilitators by example. They work side by side with the employee.

WCM is not a system or a procedure; it is a culture. It is a continually molding process of change and improvement. It is a competitive strategy for success.

In the United States, TQM has fallen into disfavor because of its analytical approach to change. The analysis process is deemed too slow to be competitive. That is primarily because

TQM utilized root cause analysis. With BT, we can revisit our use of TQM.

There are two major aspects to TQM: philosophical and operational. From the philosophical, we get guidelines and from the operational we get techniques. Traditionally, the philosophy of TQM could be stated as "Make sure you are doing the right things before you worry about doing things right." TQM focuses on careful, thoughtful analysis. However, the analysis should be creative, innovative, and innoveering oriented. It wants to make sure that we are implementing positive, goal-focused changes before we move a muscle.

TQM is an enterprise-wide change model. Some people define TQM as making the entire organization responsible for product or service quality. To some, TQM is a behavior-based philosophy of motivation and measurement. TQM does require a cultural shift for all members of an organization in that it uses an entire philosophy about how businesses should be run. TQM is filled with ideas and attitudes:

> Attitude of Desiring and Searching Out Change
> Think Culture—Move from Copying to Innovating
> Focus on the Goal
> Measurement/Motivation Planning
> Top to Bottom Corporate Strategy
> Company-wide Involvement
> Clear Definition and Implementation of Quality
> Education, Training, and Cross-Training
> Integration and Coordination
> Small, Step-by-Step Improvements

TQM implementation starts with a coordinating team, often referred to as a Quality Council. This is a team composed of high-level corporate leaders from all functional areas, usually at the vice president level. This team is appointed by the CEO and operates under his or her direction. The CEO actively directs the endeavors of the team, and is often an active team member. This Quality Council is then responsible for organizing, chartering, and measuring the performance of the other TQM teams within the organization. It oversees the installation, training, performance, and measurement of the other teams. This team aims to keep all teams focused on the corporate goal and vision.

CM works in a series of stages. The stages are:

1. Concept Creation—The development and creation of new ideas through the use of BT's innovative methods of creativity.
2. Concept Focus—The development of a target, which includes keeping your organization focused on core values and a core competency. Then, utilizing the creativity generated by Concept Creation, a set of targets is established using WCM, and a road map is developed helping us to achieve the targets.
3. Concept Engineering—This is the engineering of the ideas, converting the fuzzy concepts into usable, consumer-oriented ideas. TQM using a focused chartered team and a managed SPS process helps us to manage the concept from idea to product.
4. Concept In—This is the process of creating a market for the new concept. We transform the concept into a product, service, or system, using WCM techniques. We may utilize BT to help us develop a meaningful and effective market strategy.
5. Concept Management—Both the management of the new concepts as well as a change in the management approach (management style) is affected by the new concept. Concept Management is the integration of the first four stages of the CM process (Creation, Focus, Engineering, and In).

For more details on the CM process, read Plenert's book *Making Innovation Happen: Concept Management through Integration.*

Lean

Recently, there have been numerous articles stressing the importance of Lean in the SCM world. From these we learn about the importance of implementing Lean methodologies to:

- Eliminate waste
- Reduce cycle and flow time
- Increase capacity
- Reduce inventories
- Increase customer satisfaction
- Eliminate bottlenecks
- Improve communications

So, what is this mysterious tool referred to as "Lean"?

Lean is the Westernization of a Japanese concept that has carried several names. It has been known as the Toyota Production System (TPS), JIT, Pull Manufacturing, TQM, etc. Each of these names incorporates some aspect of Lean, and the reverse. What we know as "Lean" today is not really any of these any more. One possible definition of Lean, taken from MainStream Management, a Lean consulting company, is:

> Lean is a systematic approach that focuses the entire enterprise on continuously improving Quality, Cost, Delivery, and Safety by seeking to eliminate waste, create flow, and increase the velocity of the system's ability to meet customer demand.

What we call "Lean" today is a collection of tools and methodologies, very few of which are actually "required" in any specific Lean process. When working on a specific Lean project, part of what a Lean facilitator is required to do is to design and assemble the correct mix of tools to optimally facilitate the desired result.

Lean has developed into its own entity and along with that, it has developed its own award process, the Shingo Prize for Excellence in Manufacturing (see Chart 10.2). The Shingo award program has become the international standard for what Lean should look like. Therefore, as we look at defining Lean it would be appropriate to start with the Shingo model. A detailed write-up of the model and its principles can be found on their website, www.shingoprize.org.

The model considers both the foundational principles of Operational Excellence (see Chart 10.3) and the Transformation Process that an organization needs to go through in order

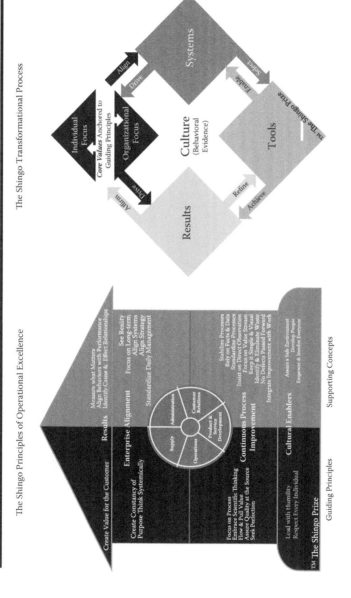

Chart 10.2 The Shingo Model

Supporting Concepts

Cultural Enablers

Assure a Safe Environment

Develop People

Empower & Involve Everyone

Continuous Process Improvement

Stabilize Processes

Rely on Facts & Data

Standardize Processes

Insist on Direct Observation

Focus on Value Stream

Keep it Simple & Visual

Identify & Eliminate Waste

No Defects Passed Forward

Integrate Improvement with Work

Enterprise Alignment

See Reality

Focus on Long-term

Align Systems

Align Strategy

Standardize Daily Management

Results

Measure what Matters

Align Behaviors with Performance

Identify Cause & Effect Relationships

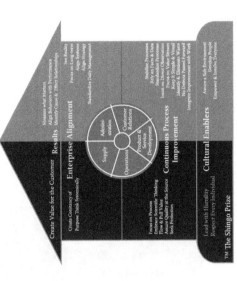

Chart 10.3 Shingo Supporting Concepts

to achieve this level of excellence. The Shingo Principles of Operational Excellence include:

- Cultural Enablers
  1. Respect every individual.
  2. Lead with humility.
- Continuous Process Improvement
  3. Seek perfection.
  4. Assure quality at the source.
  5. Flow and pull value.
  6. Embrace scientific thinking.
  7. Focus on process.
- Enterprise Alignment
  8. Think systemically.
  9. Create constancy of purpose.
- Results
  10. Create value for the customer.

Chart 10.3 highlights the Supporting Concepts that facilitate these fundamental principles.

Using these criteria as a basis for evaluation, a point system is utilized to evaluate the applicant organization on their Lean capabilities and, if their performance meets the standard, they are awarded the Shingo Award for Lean Excellence.

Lean is about team building, integration, and ownership. Someone commonly referred to as the Lean facilitator is tasked with organizing the appropriate teams and then giving them the guidance and training needed in the selected tools so that the Lean effort can progress with the greatest efficiency. The team makes the decisions about any changes in the process and it has ownership of these changes. It is the role of the facilitator to keep the team on task so it develops and implements these changes in the minimal amount of time.

Six Sigma

The term Six Sigma[*] is accurately a performance measure that was developed in order to precisely measure quality. It is

---

[*] Some of this material was developed by the author for an article in the *Encyclopedia of Management*.

focused on process variability, whereas Lean was focused on process flow. Using the Six Sigma tool we can set process goals in parts per million (PPM) in all areas of the production process. Since its origin, Six Sigma has evolved into a methodology for improving business efficiency and effectiveness by focusing on productivity, cost reduction, and enhanced quality.

Six Sigma has its roots in the efforts of Joseph Juran and W. Edwards Deming. Their programs for Zero Defects and TQM in Japan led to the adoption of the Six Sigma philosophy by Motorola. Motorola was able to achieve a 200-fold improvement in production quality and saved a reported $2.2 billion using this tool. General Electric has also become a strong proponent of Six Sigma. It claims extensive successes. GE used it during the reign of Jack Welch and this has generated global recognition. Jack Welch made Six Sigma the biggest corporate initiative in GE's history. Other users include Texas Instruments and Allied Signal. Allied took Six Sigma to an even higher level by incorporating it not just in production but also by making it a system of leadership. Other current users include JP Morgan Chase, Sun Microsystems, American Express, and Lloyds TSB. Today, Six Sigma has evolved to become a management methodology that utilizes measures as a foundational tool for business process reengineering.

The name Six Sigma comes from the statistical use of the sigma (σ) symbol, which denotes standard deviations. The six identifies the number of standard deviations around the mean. Hence, in Six Sigma we are saying that you have to go out beyond six standard deviations around the mean before you find failure. With a high enough number of sigmas (beyond six), you would approach the point of "zero defects." The sigma levels step changes, for example moving from 3σ (93% accuracy) to 4σ requires quantum leaps of improvement. A move from 3σ to 4σ is an 11 times improvement. From 4σ to 5σ is a 27 times level of improvement, and from 5σ to 6σ is a 69-fold change. Hence, moving from 3σ to 6σ is a 20,000-fold level of improvement.

At the Six Sigma level, the product failures (number of parts beyond the allowable limits) would be 3.4 PPM. This equates to 99.9997% accuracy. In today's world, 98% or 99% accuracy is considered excellent. However, Six Sigma has now become the universally recognized standard of quality.

A guiding principle of Six Sigma is that if you want some-thing to happen, you had better measure it. Unfortunately, that also means that if you measure the wrong things, you will get the wrong results. For example, measuring throughput may speed up production, but at the cost of quality. Measuring quality may increase quality, but decrease customer service. Therefore, one of the toughest challenges in Six Sigma mea-surement is to identify the measurement system that will trig-ger the correct collection of responses.

A second key principle of measures in the Six Sigma envi-ronment is that all the measures should be openly visible. Openly displaying all measures on charts and graphs is a primary motivator toward the correct response.

A third principle to remember is that the change curve applies (see Chapter 7). When change happens, performance will initially go down before it recovers and goes back up. This drop in performance is often scary, but a little patience will soon see its recovery.

A principle of success or failure in the Six Sigma world is the requirement for cultural change or change readiness. If the organization is not primed for change, then an environ-ment for change must be instilled prior to starting Six Sigma, or the project is doomed to failure. This requires training, team bonding, and team-based goal setting. The resistance that exists because of a lack of understanding of what the Six Sigma process is attempting to achieve can be avoided with proper training.

Six Sigma concentrates on measuring and improving those outputs that are critical to the customer. The tools to accom-plish this include a range of statistical methodologies that are focused on continuous improvement using a statistical think-ing paradigm. This paradigm includes the following principles:

- Everything is a process.
- All processes have variations that are inherent within them.
- Data analysis is a key tool in understanding the varia-tions in the process and in identifying improvement opportunities.

It is in the management methodology where the key, underlying benefits of Six Sigma can be found, which includes a problem-solving and process-optimization methodology. Six Sigma creates a leadership vision utilizing a set of metrics and goals to improve business results by using a systematic five-phased problem-solving methodology. Two common problem-solving project management methodologies are commonly associated with Six Sigma. The first is DMAIC (Define, Measure, Analyze, Improve, Control), and the second is DMADV (Define, Measure, Analyze, Design, Verify). We will discuss the most common, DMAIC.

Six Sigma is a measurement-based strategy that focuses on reducing variations through monitoring and measurement tools. It is based on a philosophy that holds that every process can and should be repeatedly evaluated and significantly improved, with a focus on time required, resources, quality, cost, etc. The philosophy prepares employees with the best available problem-solving tools and methodologies using the five-phased DMAIC process. Explaining each of the steps in the process in more detail, we have:

- Define—At the first stage of the process we look for and identify poorly performing areas of a company. We then target the projects with the best return and develop articulated problem and objective statements that have a positive financial impact on the company.
- Measure—At this stage, we are trying to tie down the process under consideration. Where does it start and end? What should we be measuring to identify the deviation? What data characteristics are repeatable and identifiable? What is the capability of the process? We use tools like process mapping, flow-charting, and FMEA (Failure Model Effects Analysis). We develop a baseline for the targeted area and implement an appropriate measurement system.
- Analyze—Having identified the who and what of this problem, we now target the where, when, and why of the defects in the process. We use appropriate statistical analysis tools, scatter plots, SPC and SQC, Input/Output matrixes, hypothesis testing, etc., and attempt to accurately understand what is happening in the process.

- Improve—At this point, we should have identified the critical factors that are causing failure in the process. In addition, using experiments, we can systematically design a corrective process that should generate the desired level of improvement. This improvement will then be monitored to assure success.
- Control—In the control phase, we implement process control tools that can manage and monitor the process on an ongoing basis. The DMAIC process is now in full operation, but it does not stop here. The continuous monitoring of the process will not only assure the success of this change process, but also it will identify future opportunities for improvement.

An excellent and highly recommend website is quality-digest.com, which includes several informative articles.

Summary

SCS is often a dramatic change from the current thinking and philosophy of an organization. This is a move away from traditional stability. As mentioned, if we try to stay where we are, we will be run over. Change happens to us whether we like it or not. Optimizing a Supply Chain is the process of optimizing a continuously changing environment. SCS is a key tool that drives continuous change and competitive success.

Uncontrolled and undirected change can be as disastrous as no change. What we need is to be able to stay ahead of the change curve. We need to change ourselves faster than external forces have a chance to change us. We need the change to be focused on a target. We need to maintain our corporate integrity as we institute change.

To manage change we need to incorporate change models into our business. In this chapter, we have covered some of the more popular methodologies that facilitate the change process. These change models include:

QFD
TQM

Solution to the Einstein Riddle

Houses	1	2	3	4	5
Color	Yellow	Blue	Red	Green	White
Nationality	Norwegian	Dane	Brit	German	Swede
Beverage	Water	Tea	Milk	Coffee	Beer
Smoke	Dunhill	Blends	Pall Mall	Prince	Blue Master
Pet	Cats	Horses	Birds	Fish	Dog

Chart 10.4 Solution to the Einstein Riddle

PR
CM
Lean
Six Sigma

The focus of all of these change models is:

Quality
Customer satisfaction
Continuous improvement

We also saw that some models focus on speed while others focus on analysis. Regardless of which is used, SCS requires a structured change management process in order to achieve successful implementation.

> People who live in a fish bowl don't recognize the hand that feeds them or the source of the water around them.

Now I finally offer the solution to the puzzle that I presented to you in the Preface (Chart 10.4). I hope you were successful.

Reference

Plenert, Gerhard and Shozo Hibino, *Making Innovation Happen: Concept Management Through Integration*, Delray Beach, FL: St. Lucie Press, 1997.

11

SCS Is Wonderful

You don't think your way to change
You have to work your way to change.

This last chapter is going to return us to the question of "Why Do Supply Chain Segmentation (SCS)?" (See Chart 11.1.) Up to this point, I have given the reader my personal perspective on the importance of SCS. I now want to incorporate an "industry perspective" on the important role of segmentation and some of the specific benefits it offers. An industry perspective can be gained from sources like: Supply Chain Management Review (http://www.scmr.com/) and Logistics Management (http://www.logisticsmgmt.com/).

Three articles that have valuable information are also worth reviewing. The first article I would like to consider is one written by the Aberdeen Group (www.aberdeen.com) in January 2013 by Bryan Ball titled "Demand Planning Segmentation: Getting the MAX Out of Your Business." The following quote summarizes his findings:

> Even though there are some industries that are less likely to use demand segmentation, the results indicate that those companies that do have superior performance... the results are better for companies using demand segmentation and they have a significant edge in their demand planning capabilities...

In support of these findings, he reported several interesting graphs. For example, Chart 11.2 shows segmentation usage by industry. The Wholesale and Distribution sector along with the Consumer Packaged Goods sector dominate in their usage of SCS.

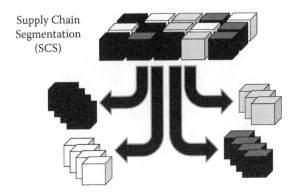

Supply Chain
Segmentation
(SCS)

Chart 11.1 SCS

Segmentation Usage by Industry	Using SCS	W/o SCS
Wholesale/Distribution	14%	4%
Consumer Packaged Goods	14%	5%
Industrial Product Mfg	12%	7%
Chemicals	7%	13%
Food/Beverage	5%	13%

Chart 11.2 Segmentation Usage by Industry

Segmentation by Business Challenge	Using SCS	W/o SCS
Optimize Service Level	74%	44%
New Product Introduction	72%	54%
Optimize Product Mix	62%	40%
Promotion Planning	61%	30%

Chart 11.3 Segmentation by Business Challenge

Moving on to another chart that came out of the Aberdeen article, in Chart 11.3 we see that users of segmentation introduced SCS primarily in order to manage Service Levels and NPIs, but Product Mix and Promotion Planning were not far behind in importance.

Metrics Showing Segmentation Benefits		
Segmentation by Business Challenge	Using SCS	W/o SCS
Current Return on Net Assets per year	17%	12%
Average Customer Service Level	90%	87%
Average Forecast Accuracy at Product Level	75%	65%

Chart 11.4 Segmentation Benefits

Sell Side Capabilities	Using SCS	W/o SCS
Accurately forecast customer demand across multiple channels and tiers	37%	22%
Perform forecast collaboration with customers and distributors	30%	13%

Chart 11.5 Sell Side Capabilities

Then the article went on to demonstrate the benefits achieved by these users of SCS. In Chart 11.4, we see that in all three key metrics, SCS performed better than those organizations without SCS.

These results were so impressive that it leaves this author wondering why any company would not want to implement SCS immediately. However, the article went on to indicate some additional interesting information. In Chart 11.5, the article focused on some of the operational benefits that can be gained by using SCS. Here we see that SCS increases forecast accuracy and performance.

Finally, in one last chart (Chart 11.6) taken from this article, we see the technology enablers that are linked to SCS. In this chart, we see how SCS facilitates forecasting and BI analytics, both of which are critical when trying to optimize performance.

Another article with valuable information is titled "Thriving in a Turbulent World: The Power of Supply Chain Segmentation."

Technology Enablers	Using SCS	W/o SCS
Statistical Demand Forecasting	71%	36%
Demand collaboration with sales for accurate forecast	66%	33%
Demand analytics and reporting/ business intelligence (BI)	60%	23%

Chart 11.6 Technology Enablers

This article was written by Dr. Janet Godsell from the Cranfield University School of Management. This article focuses on the basics of SCS and builds out a Business Alignment model. In the article, Godsell emphasizes, "The holy grail of the supply chain is to find the stable demand." In it, she offers seven steps to developing a segmented Supply Chain, which are:

1. Map out the end-to-end Supply Chain (also called value chain) to provide visibility across the business.
2. Identify the scope or "arc of integration" that the Supply Chain organization should actively manage.
3. Identify the primary customer base for the Supply Chain organization. This is the customer base at the end of the arc of integration.
4. Identify the customer demand signal to which the Supply Chain will respond, the decoupling point, and hence where strategic inventory will be held to buffer against demand: supply variability.
5. Conduct a demand profiling analysis. This is a basic two-by-two plot of demand volume vs. variability (the coefficient of variation) for each SKU within a defined region, market, or category.
6. Identify the key Supply Chain segments.
7. Develop tailored practices for each segment for each of the functions involved.

All of this fits nicely into the structure laid out in this book. Following the guidelines of this book, the reader will understand the in-depth process that needs to be executed.

If you are a business faced with the dual challenges of reducing cost whilst building the capability for growth through innovation, then supply chain segmentation has to be a serious consideration for your leadership team.

Dr. Janet Godsell

A third article worth reviewing and which supports SCS is titled "Globalization Drives Market Need for Supply Chain Segmentation: Research and Key Strategies," which was a paper and presentation sponsored by Amber Road and conducted by PRG (Peerless Research Group) on behalf of the Supply Chain Management Review and Logistics Management. The article highlighted several key points. For example:

Particularly among companies with thousands of SKUs and diverse product lines, there is a need for differentiated replenishment and logistics approaches across complex supply chains. For example, an organization may need supply chain processes that are specialized for goods with unpredictable demand, such as the latest fashion. The same organization may also provide goods with more predictable demand that require steady replenishment.

The research report goes on to state:

What we heard from our respondents is that businesses today are looking to gain greater knowledge and control over complex, multi-dimensional and global supply chains.

This article also included several invaluable tables. For example, Chart 11.7 highlights this report's findings about the Key Supply Chain Challenges. They are focused in two key areas—cost and demand variability—both of which are targeted by SCS.

Key Supply Chain Challenges	
Rising Transportation Rates	50%
Fluctuations in Customer Demand	50%
Increasing Customer Expectations	42%
Global Economic Turmoil and Uncertainty	38%
Changing Regulatory Requirements	35%

Chart 11.7 Key Supply Chain Challenges

How Supply Chain Capabilites Are Segmented	
By Product	57%
By Line of Business	48%
By Time of Delivery	38%
By Lead Time	35%
By Cost	27%
By Speed to Market	18%
By Supply Risk	14%

Chart 11.8 How SCS Is Segmented

The Importance of Supply Chain Segmentation	
Very Important	28%
Important	56%
Neutral	11%
Not Very Important	4%
Not at all Important	1%

Chart 11.9 SCS Importance

A second interesting table is shown in Chart 11.8. Here we see the types of segmentation structures used by various organizations. There are no surprises here; just confirmation that we need to focus on the correct areas that require further SCS analytics.

A third chart taken from this article and which is shown here as Chart 11.9 helps us see how this research report's respondents reacted to the importance of SCS. Here we see that 84 percent of those surveyed classify SCS as Important or Very Important.

A last chart from this article that is useful for the readers of this book is shown as Chart 11.10. In this chart, we see the types of tools that are utilized for SCS optimization in each of the SCS segments. These are the same types of tools that the readers would utilize within their own organizations as they look for ways to define the planning and scheduling methodology of each of their respective segments.

Solutions for Managing a Segmentation Strategy	
Transportation Management	52%
Order Fulfillment or Order Management	47%
Sales and Operations Planning (S&OP)	45%
Inventory Optimization (Network Design)	44%
Supply Chain Performance Management (Analytics)	44%
Demand Planning	44%
Strategic Sourcing	43%
Warehouse Management	41%
Supply Chain Visibility/Event Management	40%
Procurement	40%
Supply Chain Risk Management	36%
Product and Distribution Planning	35%
Trade Compliance	22%
Labor/Workforce Management	20%

Chart 11.10 Managing a SCS Strategy

The research report ends with a warning:

Effective operation of supply chain segmentation requires greater optimization of sourcing and distribution, improved order fulfillment procedures, greater accuracy in demand planning, and stronger supplier management practices.

I could also offer a long list of success stories, but most of that content has already been incorporated in this book within the case examples. However, one very specific set of results that I recently experienced is shown in Chart 11.11. In this chart, we see a dramatic reduction in the number of stock-outs, which is the direct result of an improved and focused (SCS) planning and scheduling system. Looking at the overall numbers, we have a 95 percent reduction in the number of stock-outs while simultaneously achieving a 50 percent reduction in inventory levels.

This last case is an interesting example of the types of improvements that can be achieved using segmentation. Some additional Measures of Success include:

- 80 percent reduction in the use of manual forecasting
- 100 percent policy driven inventory modeling in system
- Increased forecast accuracy as demonstrated by the reduction of stock-outs
- Reduction in inventory while maintaining or increasing service levels

**SCS Performance Gains by
Segmentation Planning Method**

Segment Name	Performance Gain	
	Inventory $$	# of Stock-Outs
NPI	19%	100%
OIL (Stable)	64%	99%
Min/Max (Declining)	–8%	96%
BTO/ EOL	94%	87%
Overall	50%	95%

Chart 11.11 SCS Performance Gains

- Reduction in obsolescence
- Simplification of entire planning systems

Moving away from this specific example, we can generalize about SCS. We see that the positive effects include:

1. Less work/effort in the planning process
2. Significant on-hand inventory cost reductions in High Demand/Low Variability products
3. Significant obsolete inventory cost reductions in BTO and EOL
4. Significant stock-out reductions in all sectors
5. 80 percent of the SKUs should be medium or low touch in the production planning process
6. Significant overall inventory turns ratio reduction
7. New, stronger focus on data quality and data accuracy
8. Increased planning visibility/event management
9. Increased on-time delivery performance
10. Improved OTTR (On Time to Requested Due Date)
11. Increased margins
12. Increased revenue

On the negative side, the NPI products tend to have minimal or no product planning improvement because they continue to be managed manually using tools like S&OP.

Segmentation Variability Spectrum

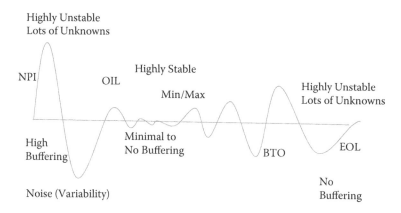

Chart 11.12 Segmentation Variability

Segmentation Volume Spectrum

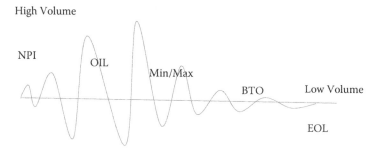

Chart 11.13 Segmentation Volume

Another way to look at the performance and results of segmentation is shown in Charts 11.12, 11.13, and 11.14. In the first of these three charts, Chart 11.12, we see the effects of product forecast variability as we migrate through the life of a product. This variability directly influences what type of planning and scheduling system would have the most optimal performance results. We see the worst level of variability during the NPI stage where very little is known about the demand pattern for the new product. As the market becomes familiar with the product, a stable demand pattern forms. Then, as

Segmentation Margin Spectrum

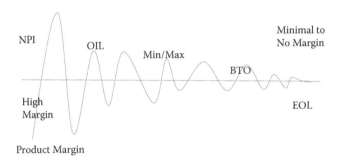

Chart 11.14 Segmentation Margin

other product alternatives emerge, demand variability creeps back in until we close the product out at the end of its life.

From Chart 11.12, we also see that the level of buffering that the product requires varies with the life stage in which we find the product. We have higher buffering during the early stages and less buffering later in the product's life when we are trying to avoid obsolete inventories.

The second of the three charts, Chart 11.13, focuses on the sales volume of the product. In this case, we see that the highest sales volume occurs during the stable product stages of the product's life.

The third chart (Chart 11.14) focuses on the product margin. In this chart, we see that margin is highest at the early product lifecycle stages and declines significantly as the product approaches EOL. It is during the OIL stages, where volume is highest, that the enterprise maximizes its cash flow taking advantage of its high margins.

By this point, the reader should have a strong understanding of segmentation, why it is important, and how it is implemented. The reader should also understand the advantages of SCS. A few summary topics that should still be discussed include:

- Defining Segmentation Goals
- Segmentation Governance
- The Effect of SCS on the Organization

Defining Segmentation Goals is a critical piece of the overall SCS successful implementation. It is the first big piece of constructing a successful segmentation environment. It was also one of the first topics of this book. However, it is important to come back to this topic because the fuzziness of the topic causes it to be ignored. Review the sections on setting goals and defining metrics. Then establish a measurable set of goals that will clearly define the success of the SCS project.

Segmentation governance goes along with setting goals. Governance is the monitoring of the progress of the SCS implementation. We can establish dashboards and scorecards that monitor our progress with respect to the goals and metrics that we established. Only with this type of monitoring are we able to tweak our SCS environment and increasingly demonstrate its success.

Finally, the effect of SCS on the organization can be quite dramatic. Obviously, it redefines the roles of the entire planning organization, focusing it heavily on the NPI and EOL products, and letting the automated system monitor the other stages of a product's life. Additionally, the IT organization is dramatically affected because of the SCS software add-on that will be required. Then there is also the integration of the new software into the overall ERP environment. The analytics organization is dramatically affected as well. It will be up to them to monitor and provide recommendations to the SCS structure. The business unit of the company will be looking at customer service levels differently and will spend less time monitoring inventory levels with this new SCS approach. And the list goes on, demonstrating changes throughout the organization.

Summary

This chapter has focused on SCS impact. In this final chapter, we have reviewed the benefits of SCS and the potential organizational changes that can be expected because of implementing an SCS structure. This chapter has also demonstrated that SCS is considered a world-class best practice by many of the major research organizations in the world. Now it is your turn. Are you ready to transform your organization by executing world-class changes through SCS and its corresponding analytics?

It's better to wear out than to rust out.

Index

W

Z

For Product Safety Concerns and Information please contact our EU
representative GPSR@taylorandfrancis.com Taylor & Francis Verlag GmbH,
Kaufingerstraße 24, 80331 München, Germany

Printed and bound by CPI Group (UK) Ltd, Croydon, CR0 4YY

08/05/2025

01864370-0016